Harriston and Clifford Ontario in Colour Photos, Saving Our History One Photo at a Time

Photography
by Barbara Raué
2014

Series Name:
Cruising Ontario

Book 105: Harriston and Clifford

Cover photo: Clifford – see Page 27

Series Name: Cruising Ontario
Saving Our History One Photo at a Time
in colour photos

Other Books by Barbara Raue

Coins of Gold

Arrows, Indians and Love

The Life and Times of Barbara
Volume 1: Inventions That Have Enhanced My Life
Volume 2: Entertainment That I Have Enjoyed
Volume 3: East Coast Trips
Volume 4: Olympics Have Always Intrigued Me
Volume 5: Wonders of the World
Volume 6: Caribbean Cruises We Have Enjoyed
Volume 7: Animals
Volume 8: Storms and Other Major Disasters in My Lifetime
Volume 9: Wars, Terrorist Attacks and Major Disasters

The Cromwell Family Book

Laura Secord Discovered

Daddy Where Are You?

Visit Barbara's website to view all of her books
http://barbararaue.ca

Harriston

Harriston is a community in Wellington County located at the headwaters of the Maitland River. In the summer of 1845, the first non-Aboriginal settlers arrived in the area and the Crown made land available for sale in the region in 1854.

The town was named after Archibald Harrison, a Toronto farmer who was granted land along the Maitland River in 1854. Harrison's brothers George and Joshua built several mills in the area and the community soon grew.

A post office was established in 1856. The southern road leading to Harriston was graveled in 1861, opening easier access to the larger markets of Guelph, Hamilton, and Toronto. By 1867, the village contained many businesses including wagon works and blacksmith shops.

The town became a prosperous commercial and farm-implement manufacturing centre following the construction of the Wellington Grey and Bruce Railway, completed to Harriston in 1871. A telegraph link to the community followed soon after. A second rail line, the Toronto, Grey and Brue Railway, intersected the village in 1873.

Harriston was incorporated as a village in 1872, and as a town in 1878. In 1882, the Grand Trunk Railway began shipping through Harriston. A Carnegie Library opened in Harriston in 1908.

Beginning in the late 1860s, Harriston's citizens began to create friendly service organizations parallel to, as well as outside, of religious groups. In 1868, the Loyal Orange Institution opened a Harriston Lodge; in 1871, the Freemasons established a Lodge. Other groups followed, such as the Independent Order of Oddfellows (1879), and the Independent Order of Good Templars (active by 1874) and the Royal Templars of Temperance (active by 1900).

The Harriston Minto Agricultural Society was founded in 1859 and continues to operate an annual fall fair on the third weekend in September

Clifford

Clifford is a community in the Town of Minto in Wellington County. The village of Clifford was founded around 1855 as Minto Village. After the opening of the post office in 1856, the settlement was renamed Clifford by the first postmaster Francis Brown after Clifford in West Yorkshire, England. Clifford was incorporated as a village in 1873.

Clifford is home to Wightman Telecom. The Wightman family has owned and operated a communication system in Clifford since 1908. The company is now involved in high speed fiber-optic internet, cable, and telephone throughout mid-western Ontario.

Table of Contents

Harriston

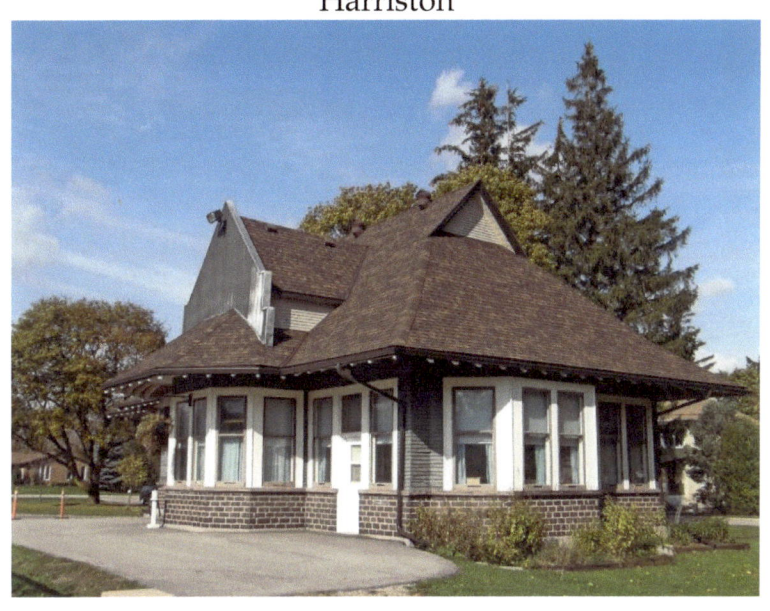

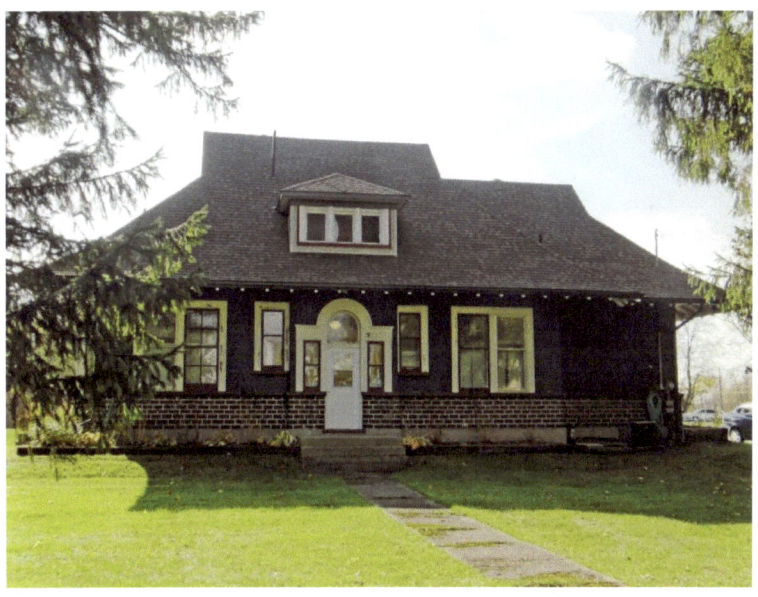

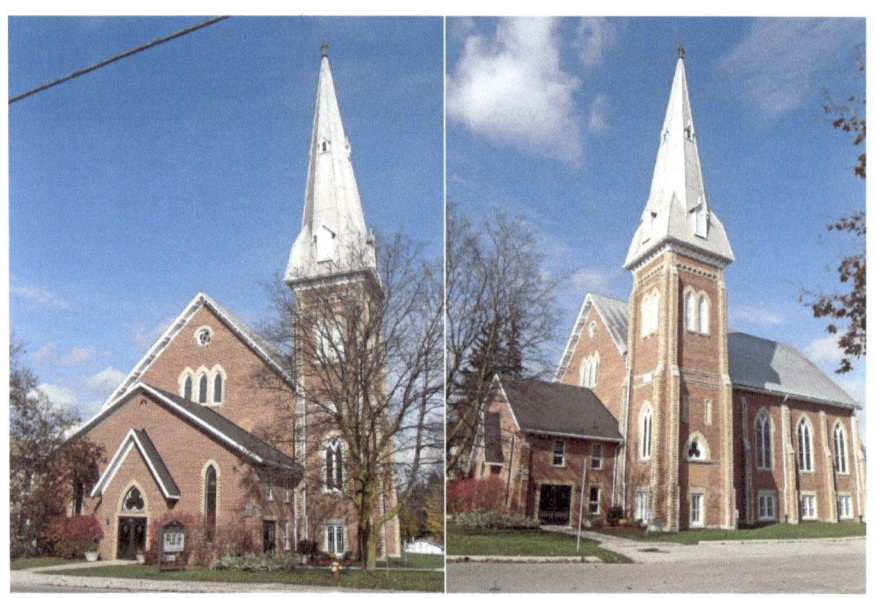

Knox Presbyterian Church – dedicated June 27, 1877
Buttresses, lancet windows, dichromatic brickwork

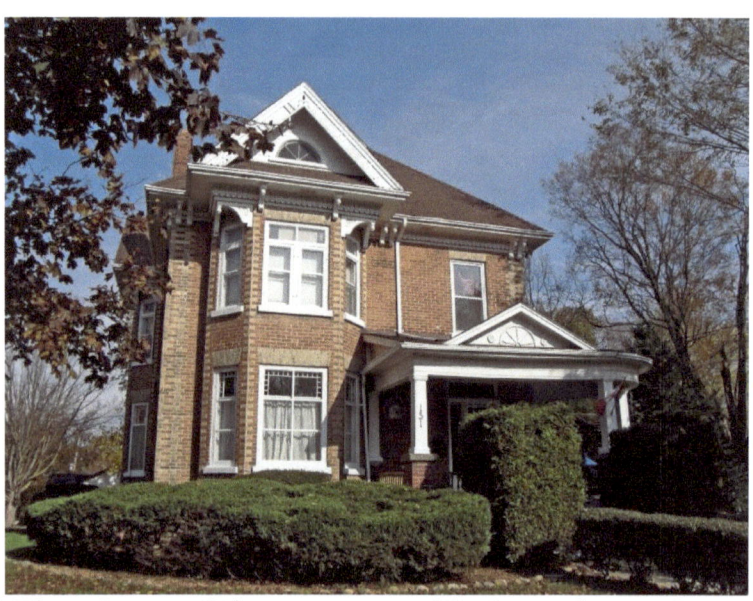

151 Elora Street – 2½ storey tower-like bays, fretwork, corner
quoins, cornice brackets, pediment above verandah

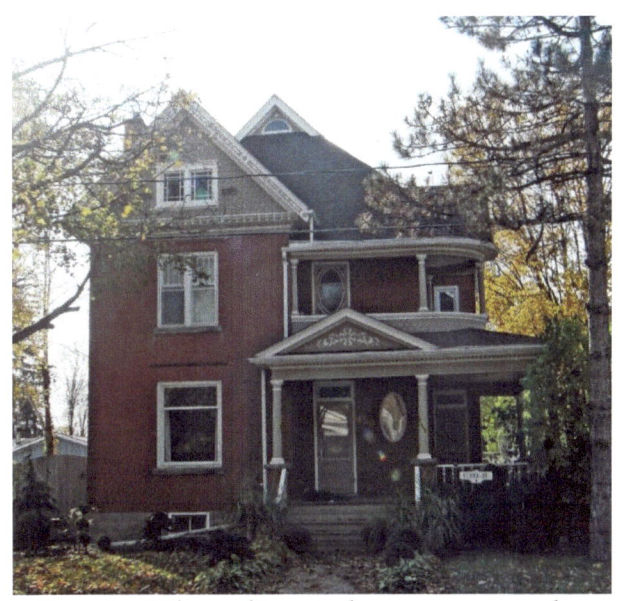

#150 Elora Street – Edwardian style, wraparound verandah on both levels, pediment

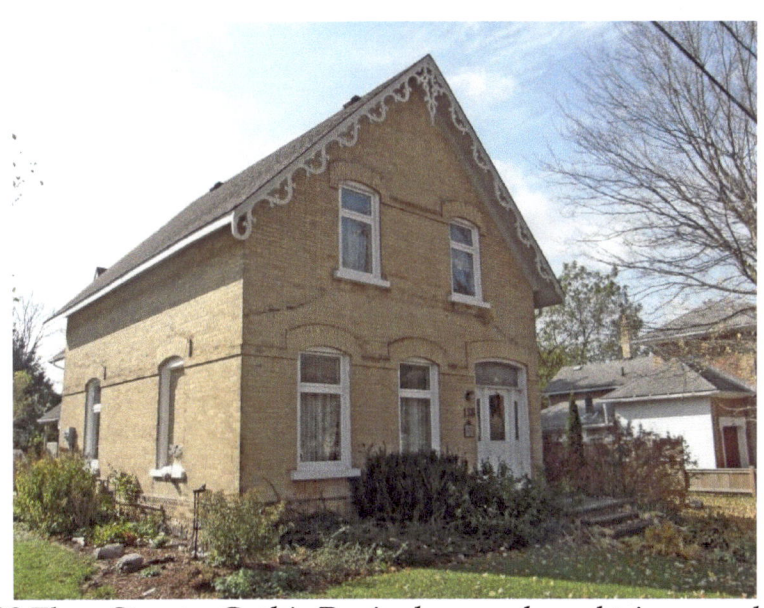

138 Elora Street – Gothic Revival, verge board trim on gable
William Gordon, Cheesemaker - 1875

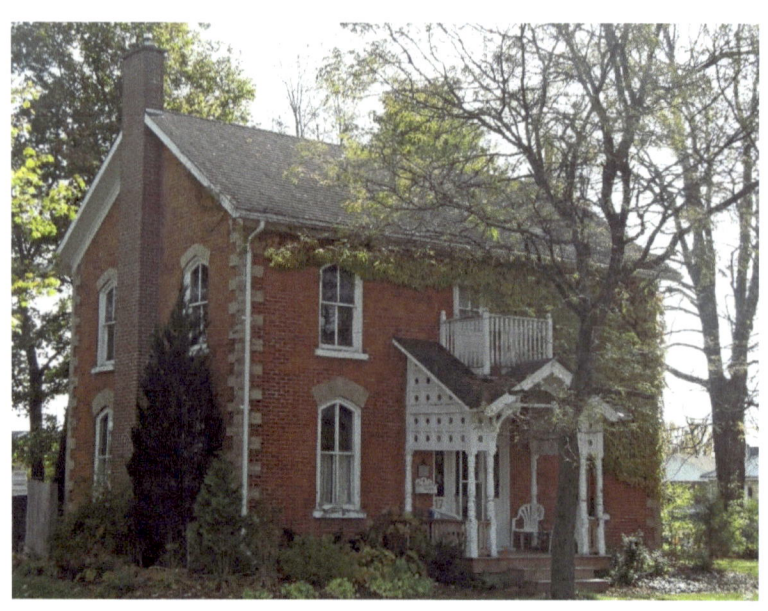

#17 - Gothic Revival, corner quoins, balcony above entranceway – heritage building

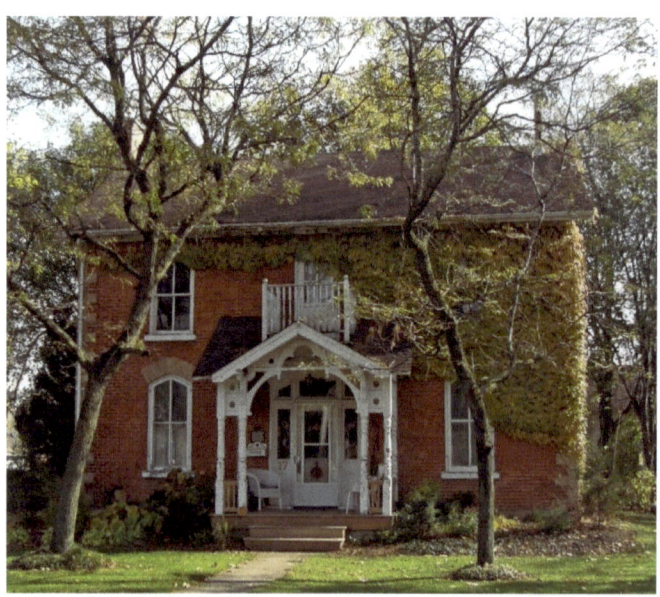

J.A.W. Hatton, Barrister – 1877

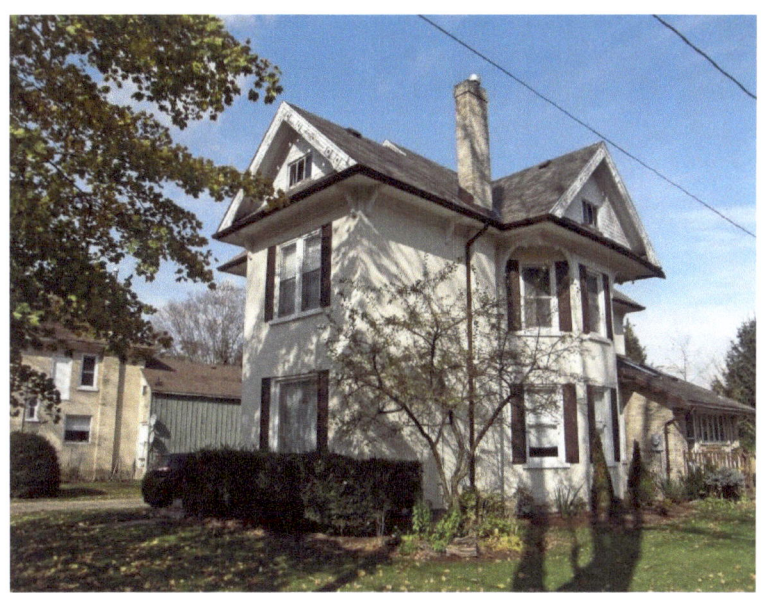

Edwardian style – two-storey tower-like bay

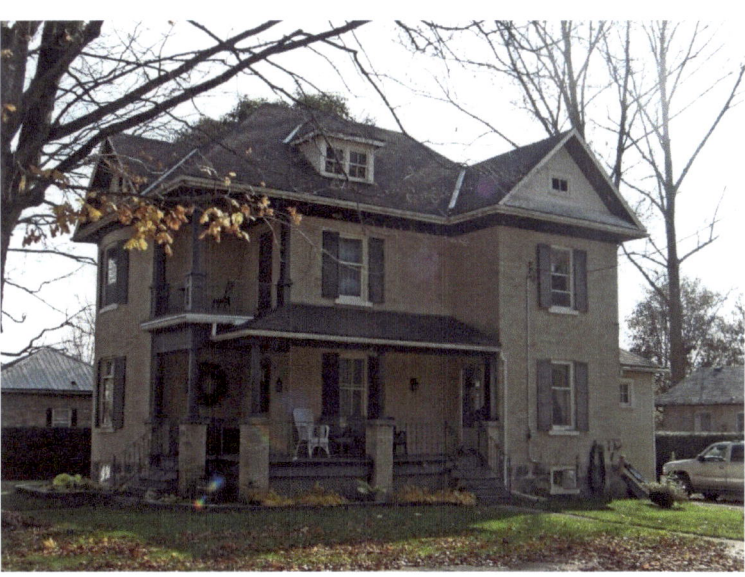

Yellow brick, heritage building, dormer in attic

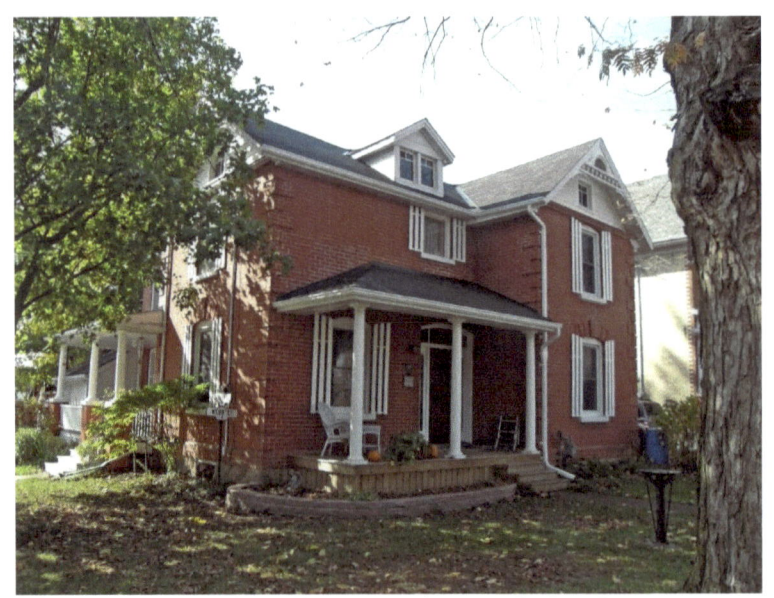

#138 – Nathan Fallis, Cheesemaker – 1879 – dormer in attic

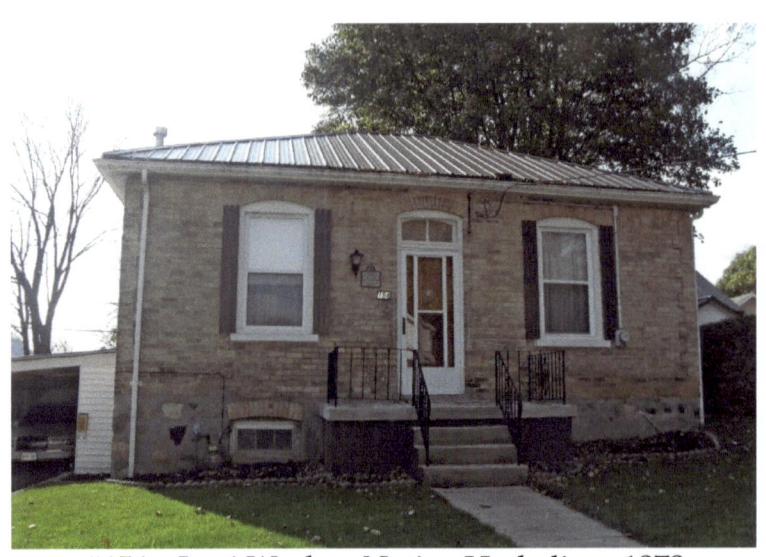

#154 – Levi Wesley, Native Herbalist – 1878
Italianate style cottage

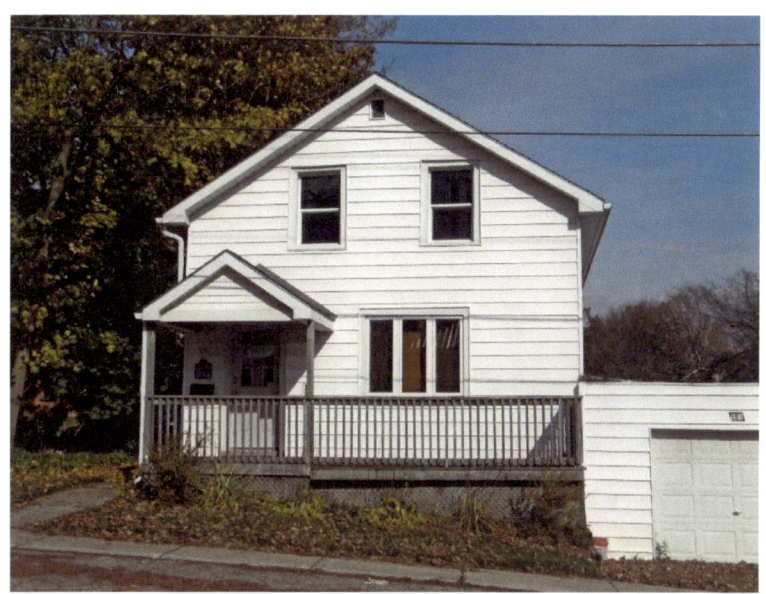

#151 – William Caldwell, Pottery Shop – 1879
Gothic Revival - pediment

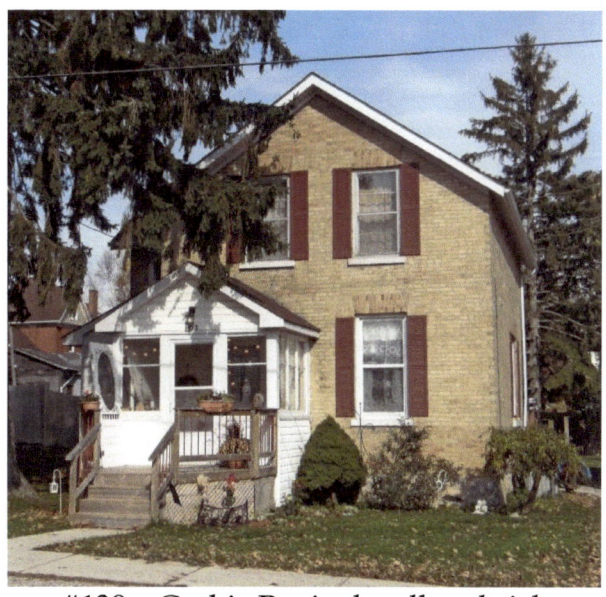

#139 – Gothic Revival, yellow brick

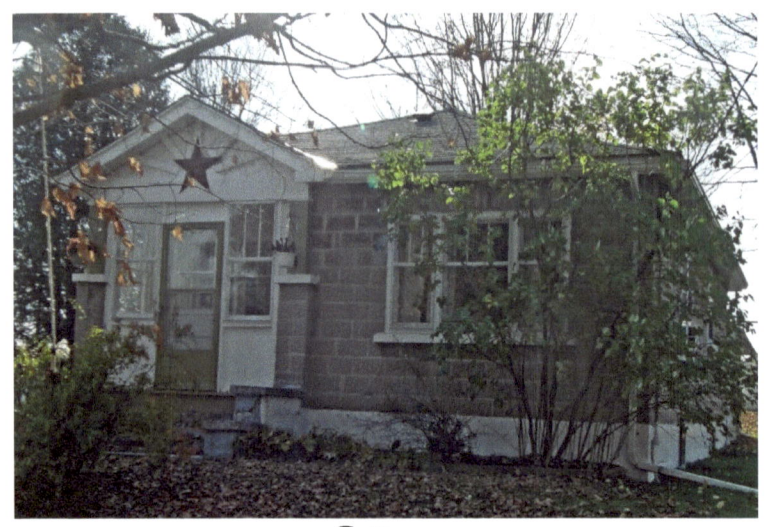

Cottage

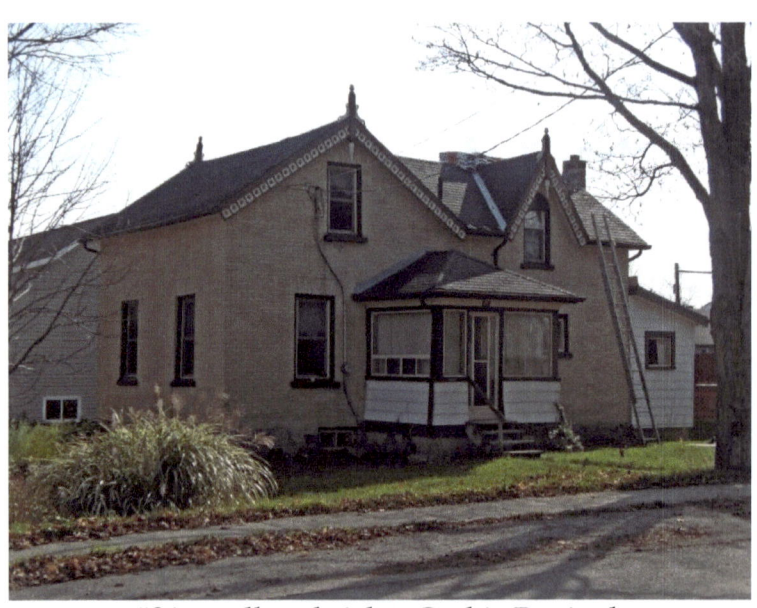

#31 – yellow brick – Gothic Revival,
verge board trim on gables with finials

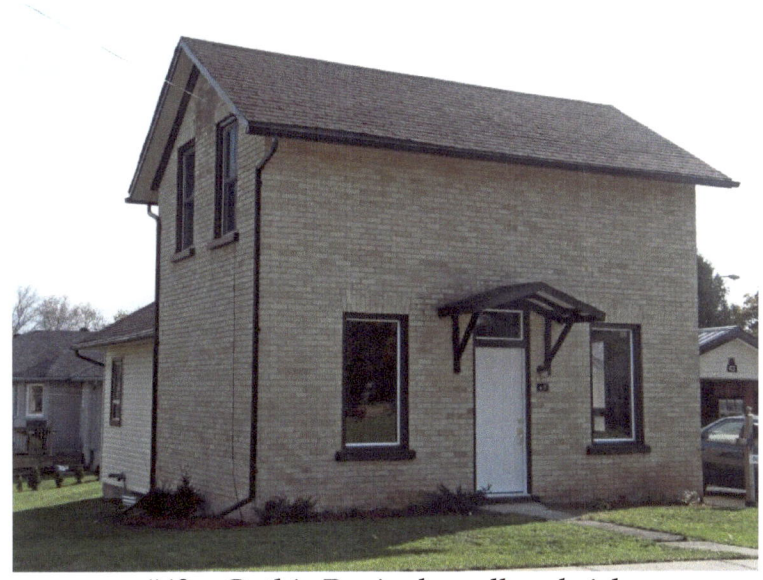

#43 – Gothic Revival – yellow brick

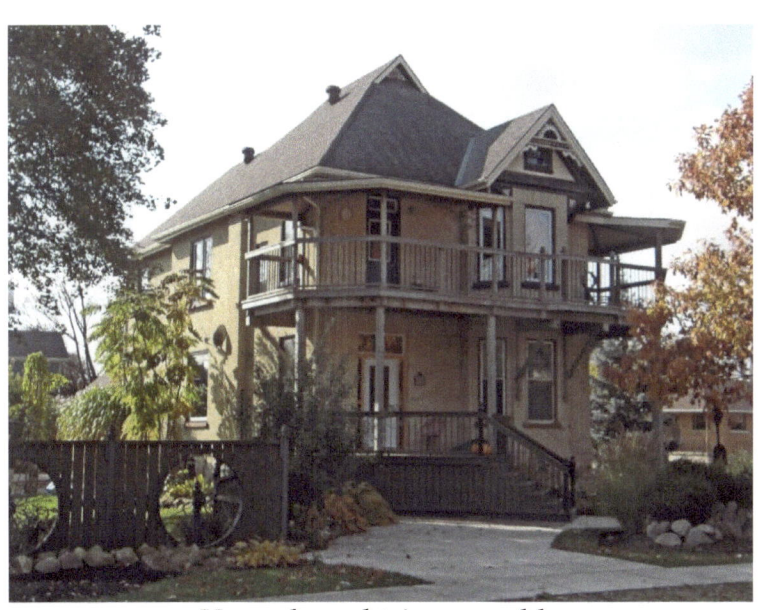

Verge board trim on gable

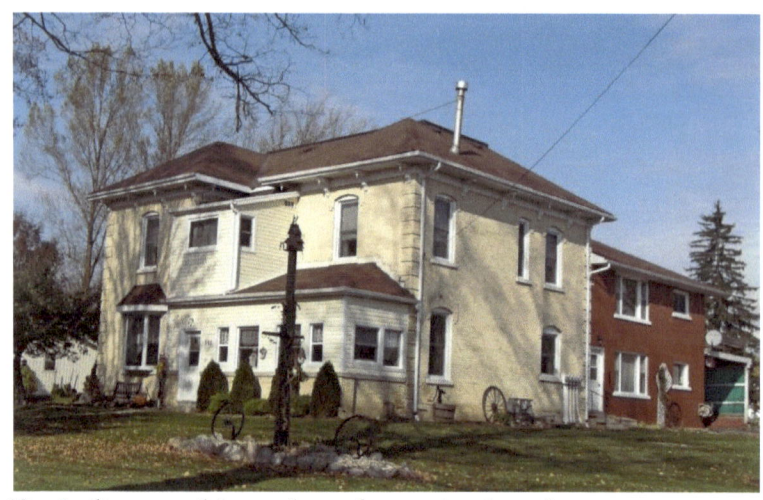

#163 - Italianate, hipped roof, cornice brackets, corner quoins

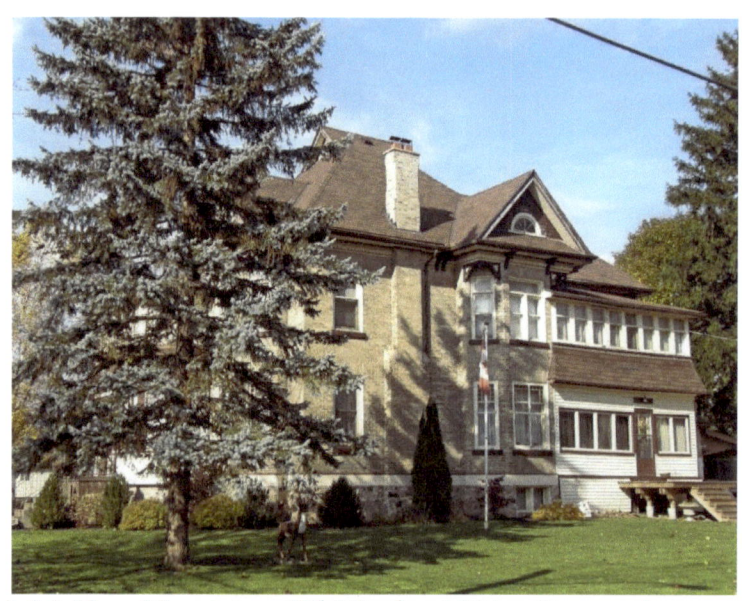

J.M. McKay, Harriston Oil Works, 1894 – Queen Anne style

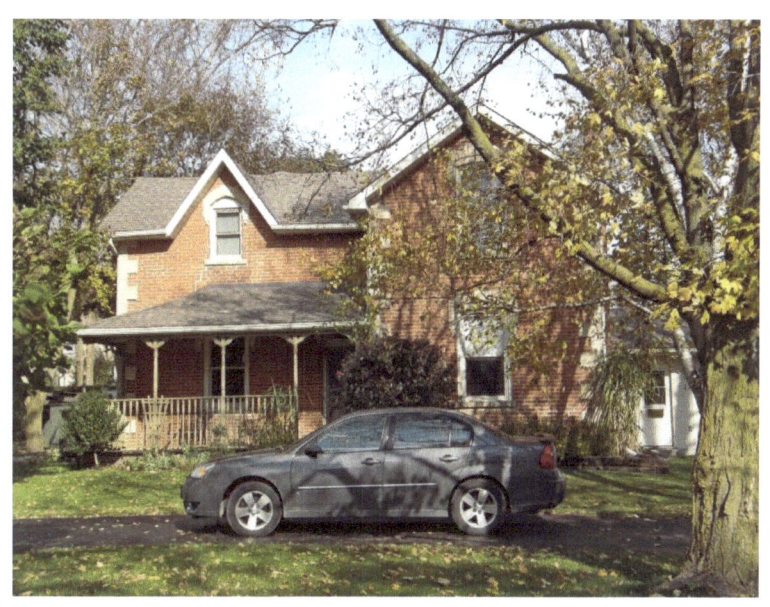

Gothic Revival, corner quoins

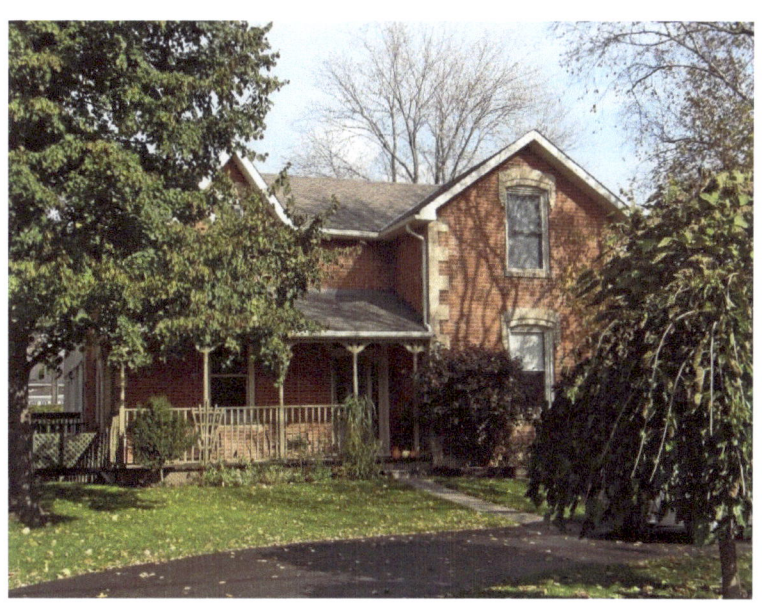

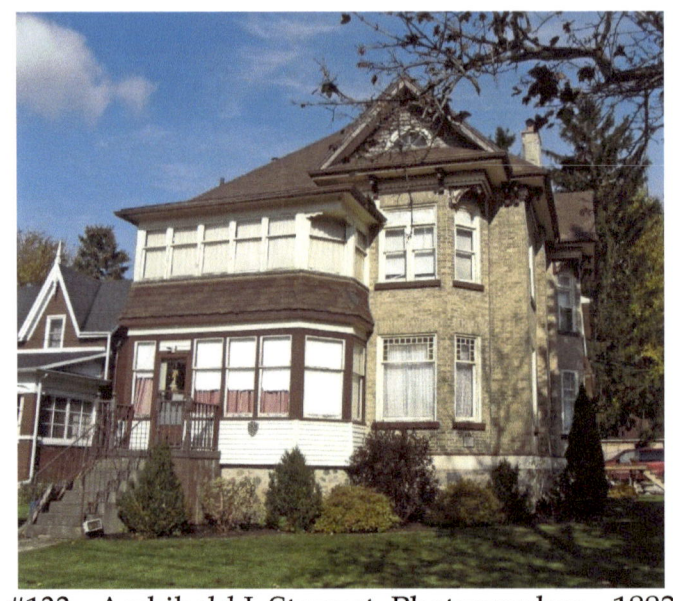

#133 - Archibald J. Stewart, Photographer – 1882
Queen Anne style

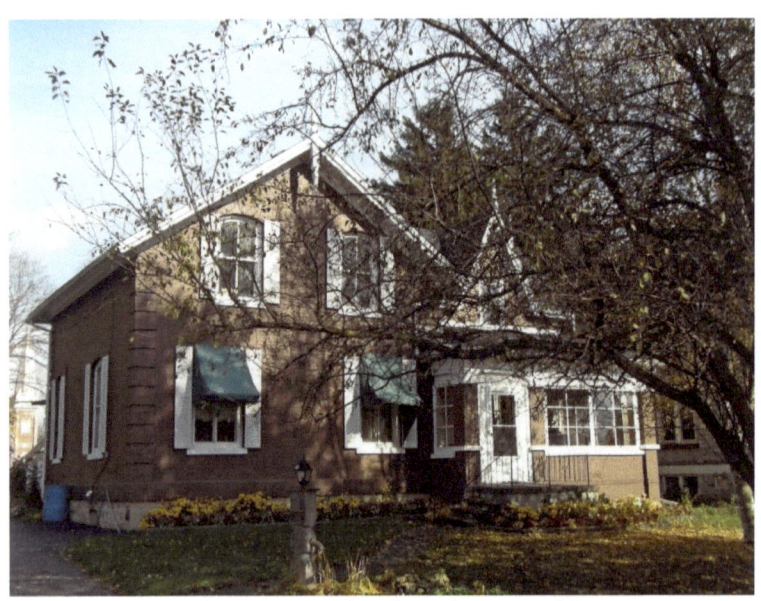

Gothic Revival – finials on gables

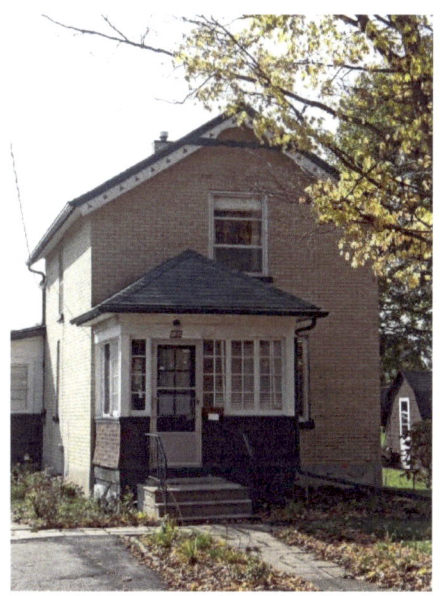

#132 – Gothic Revival

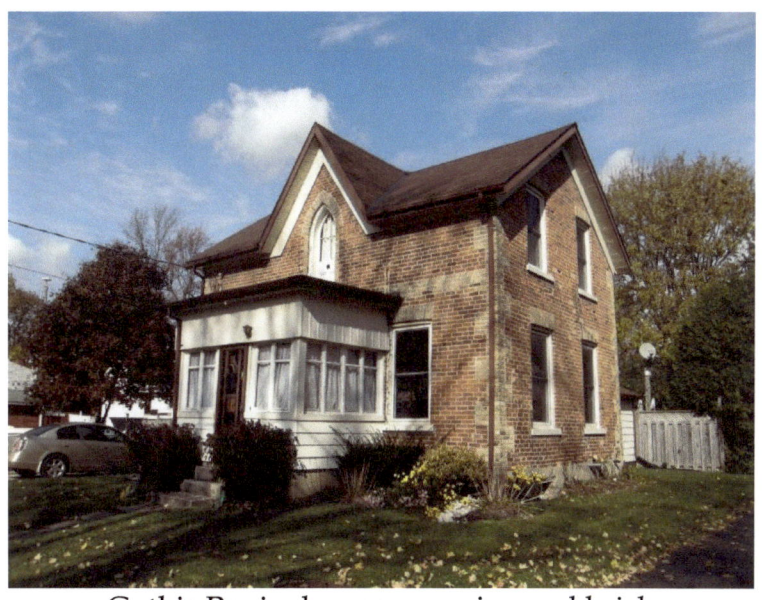

Gothic Revival, corner quoins, red brick

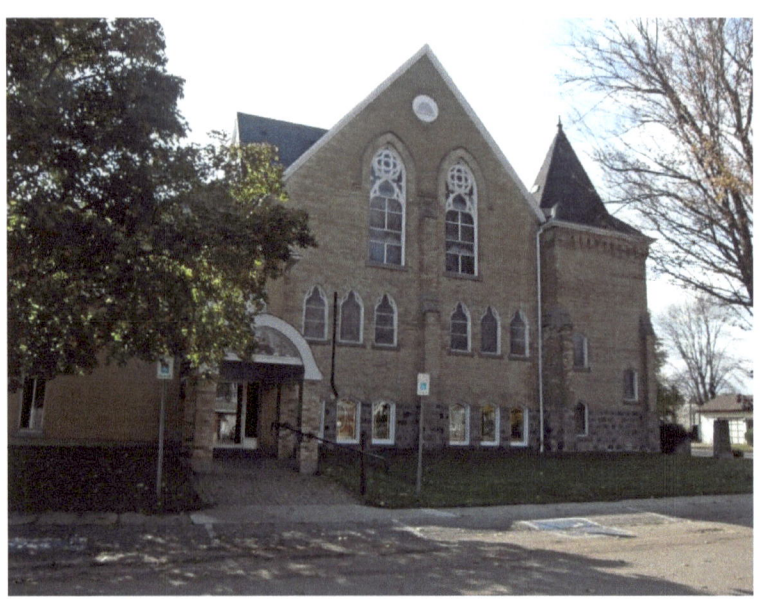

Harriston United Church – bevelled dentil moulding, yellow brick, buttresses, cobblestone basement walls

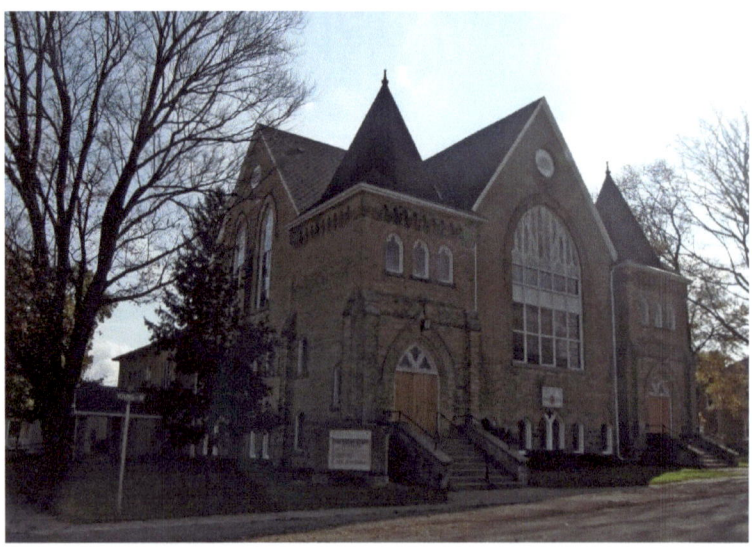

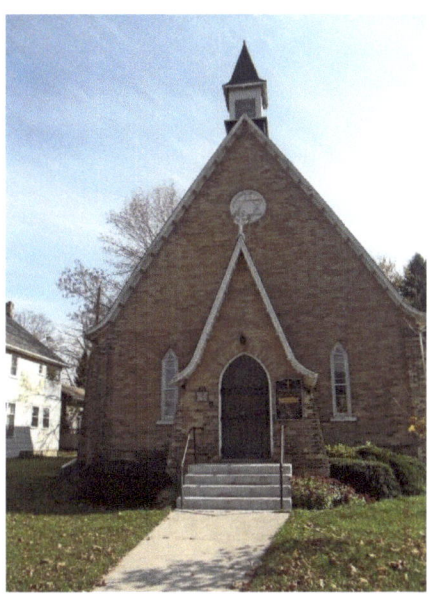

St. George's Anglican Church
First service – December 25, 1870

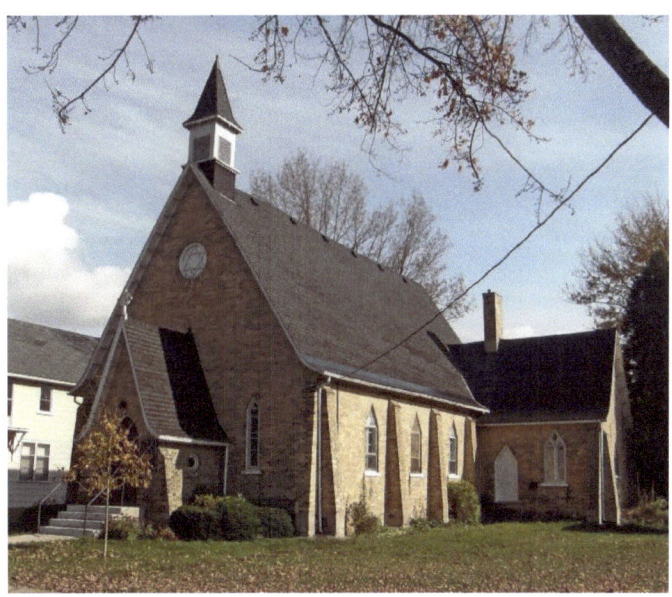

Gothic – buttresses, cupola

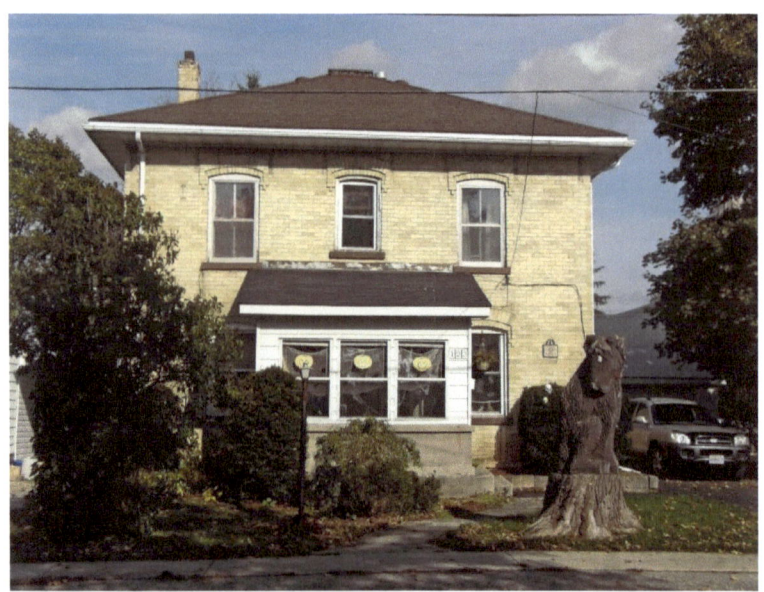

#123 – Alexander McDougall, Contractor – 1874
W. A. Harvey, M.D. – 1885 – Italianate, hipped roof

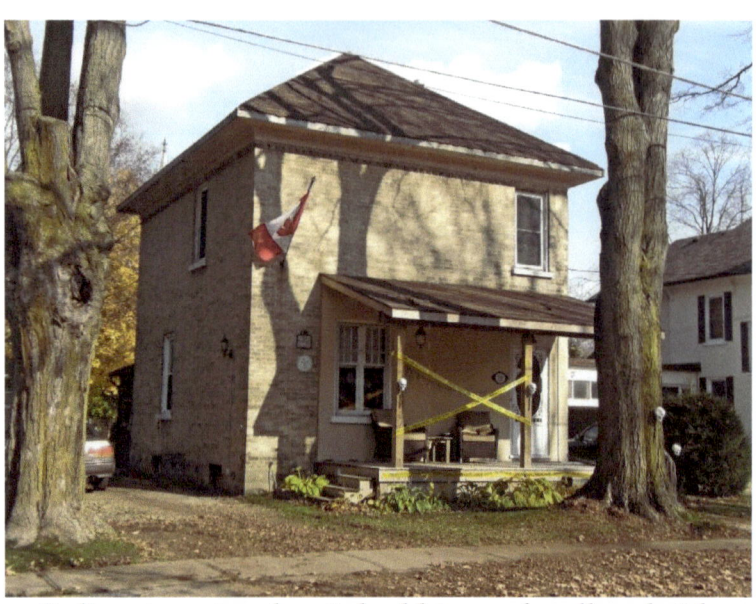

Italianate – steeply pitched hip roof, yellow brick
William Beatty, House Builder - 1895

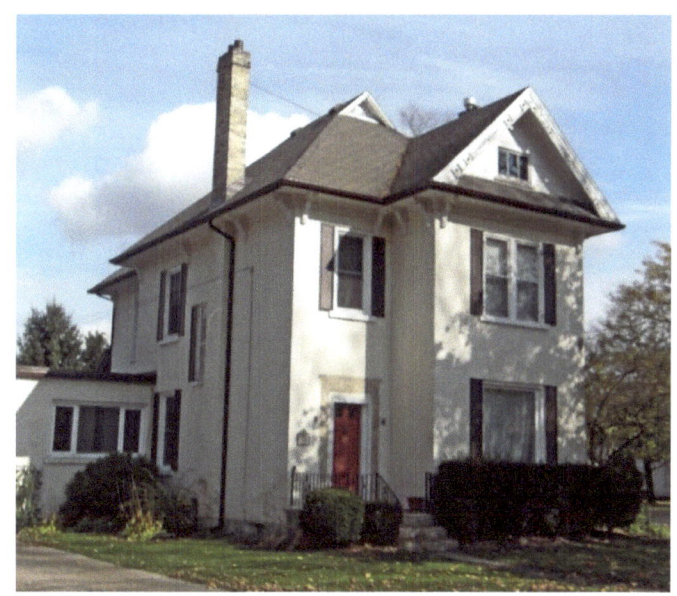

Joseph Lavery, Retired Farmer – 1895
Edwardian, cornice brackets

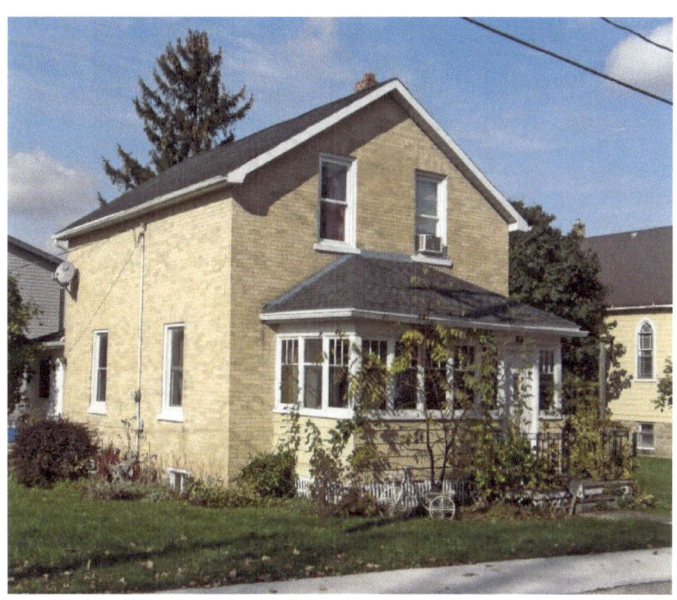

Gothic Revival

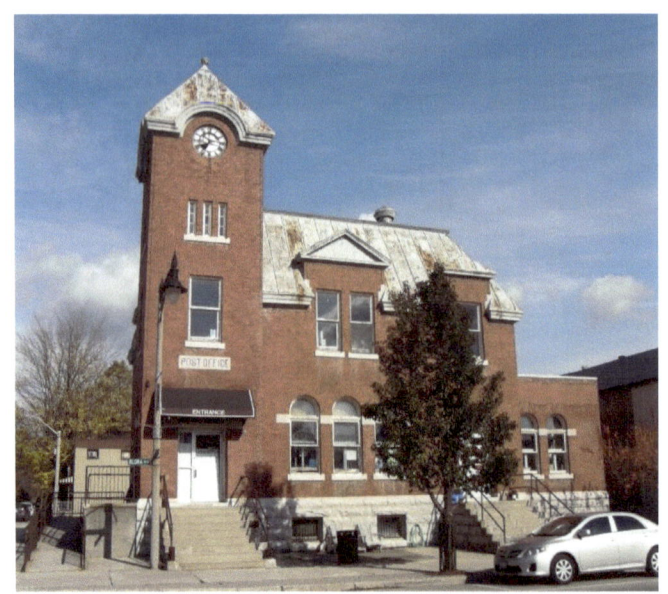

Elora Street – Post Office, clock tower, red brick

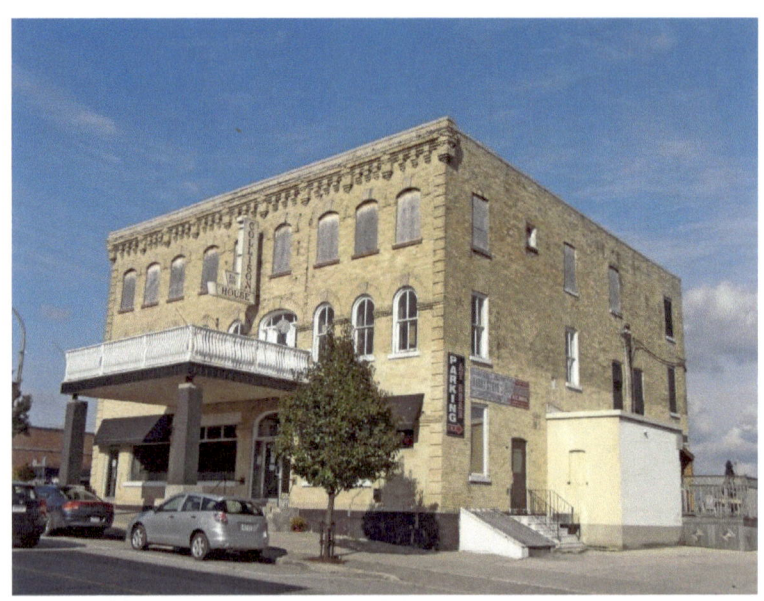

Bevelled dentil moulding, corner quoins,
balcony above entrance, yellow brick

Clifford

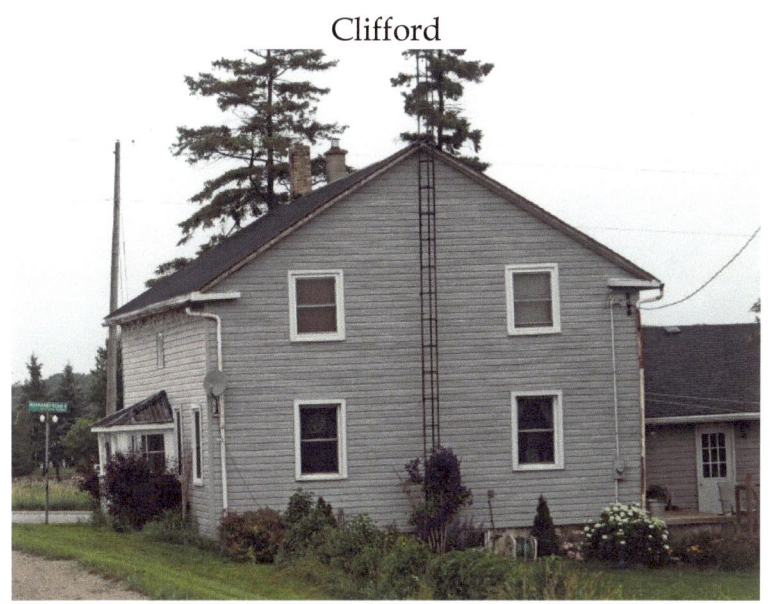

Normanby Road 9

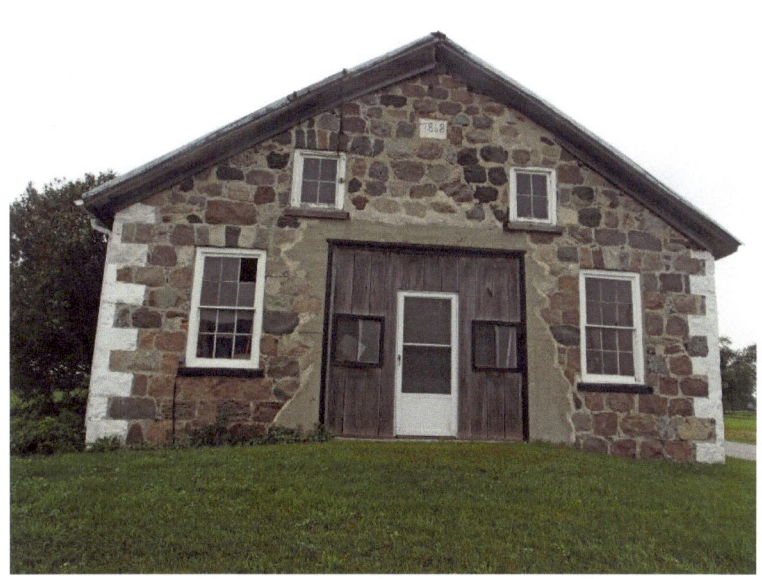

1868 – cobblestone architecture – Gothic style

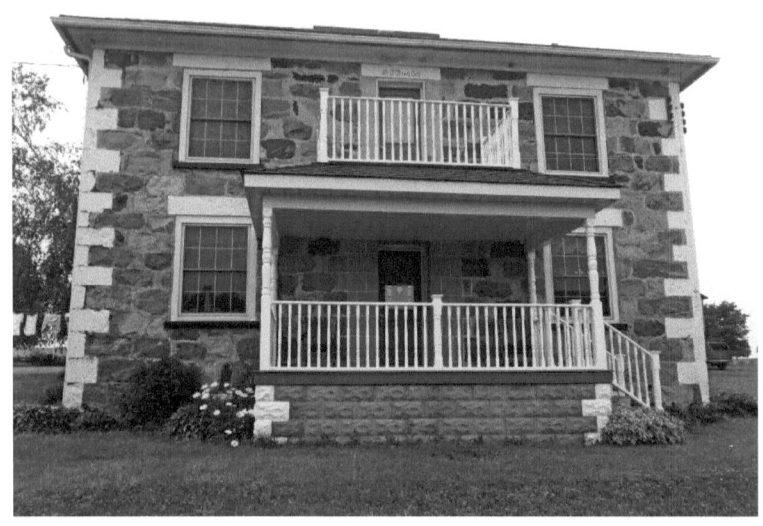

1868 – cobblestone, corner quoins, balcony on second floor

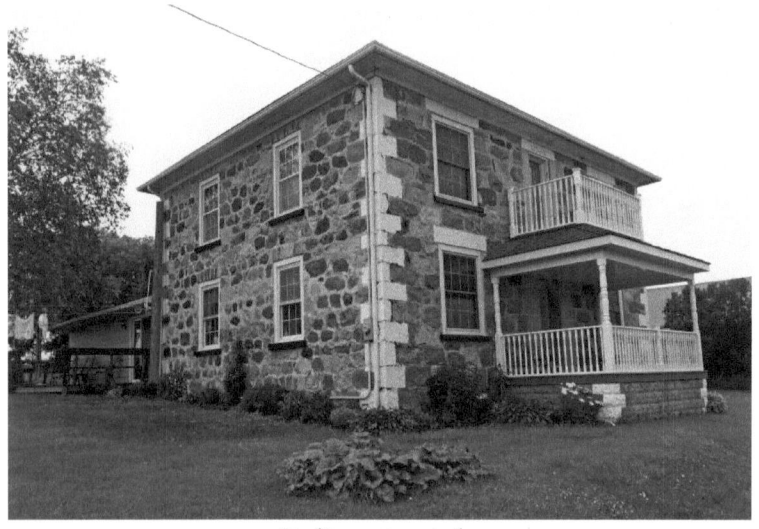

Italianate style

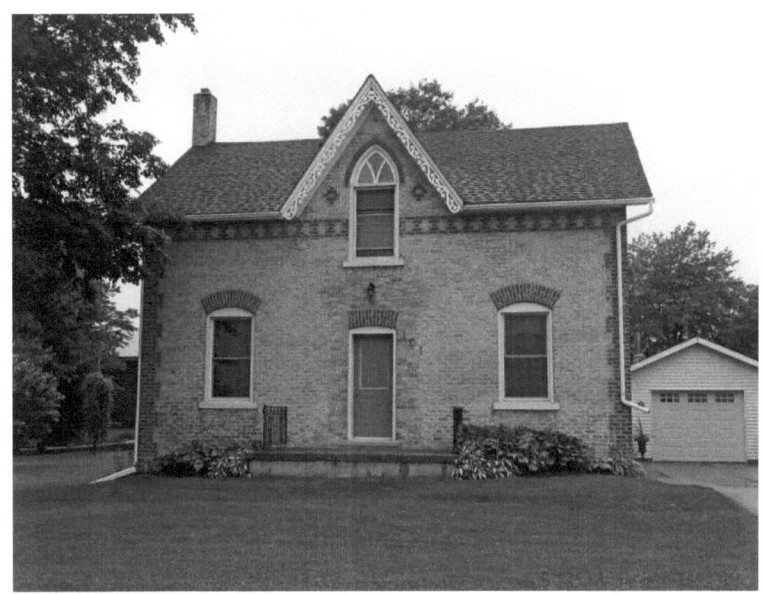

#101 - Gothic Revival, dichromatic brickwork, verge board trim

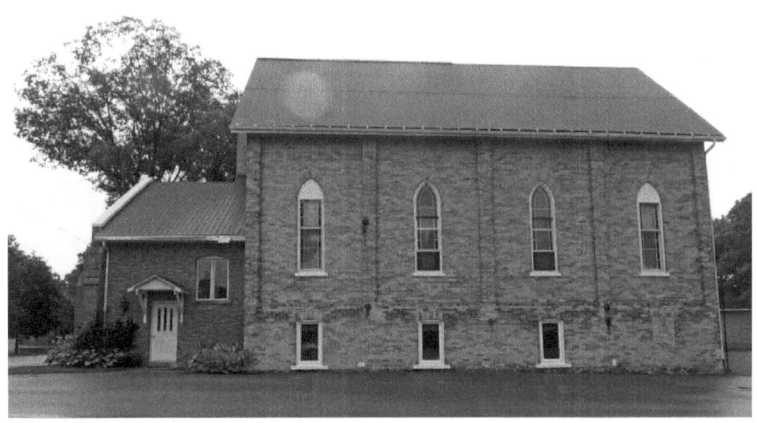

St. Johns Evangelical Lutheran Church – lancet windows, pilasters, bevelled dentil moulding below cornice

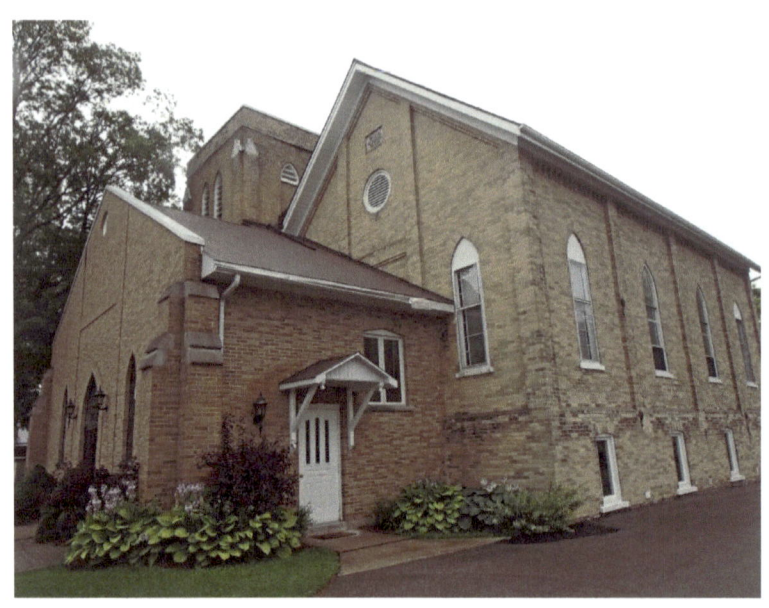

St. Johns Evangelical Lutheran Church – lancet windows

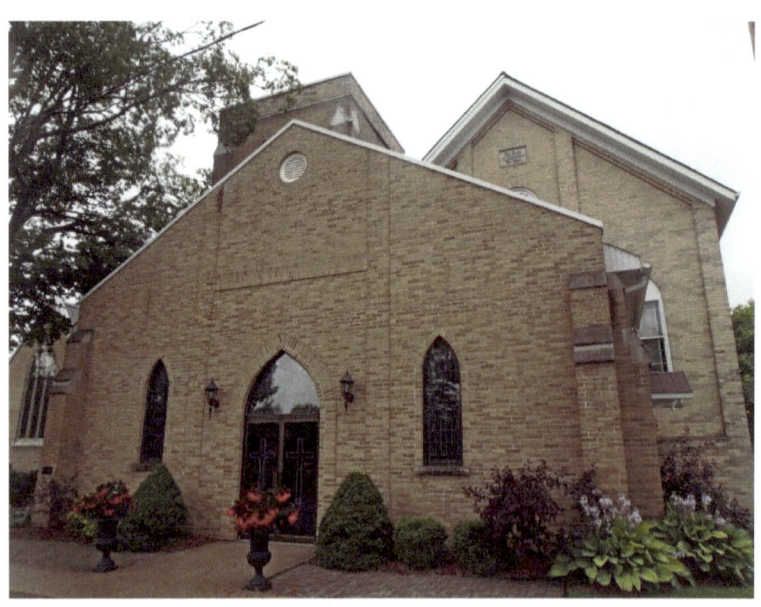

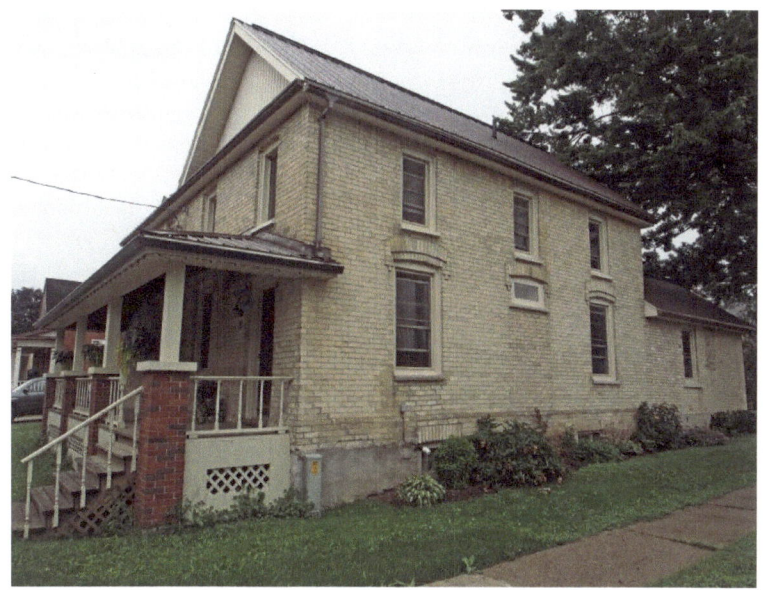

#12 – yellow brick - Gothic

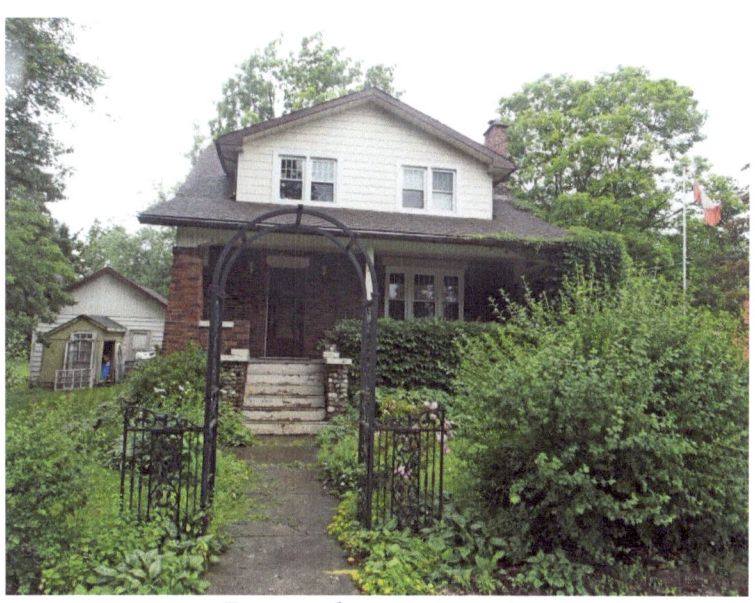

Larger dormer in attic

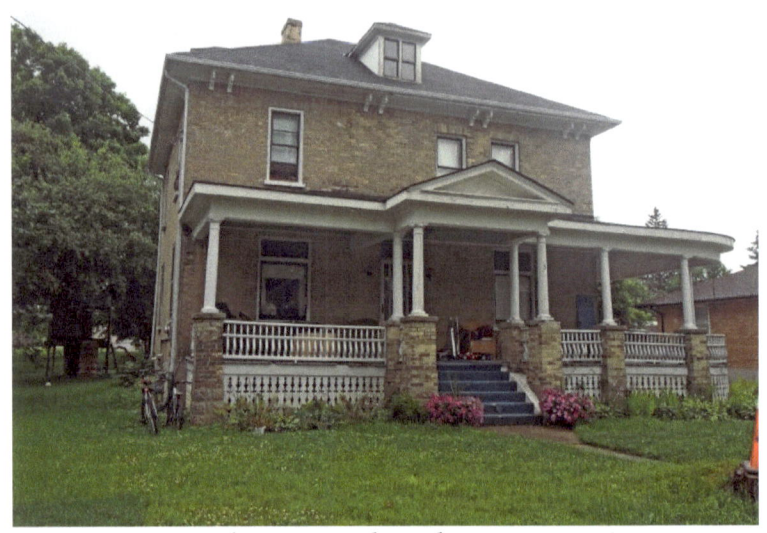

#3 - Italianate style – dormer in attic, cornice brackets, pediment

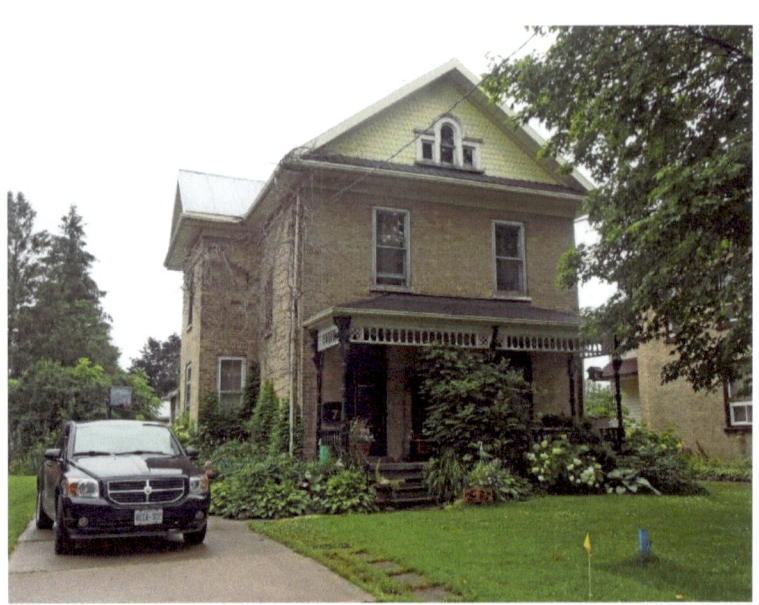

Edwardian style – Palladian window

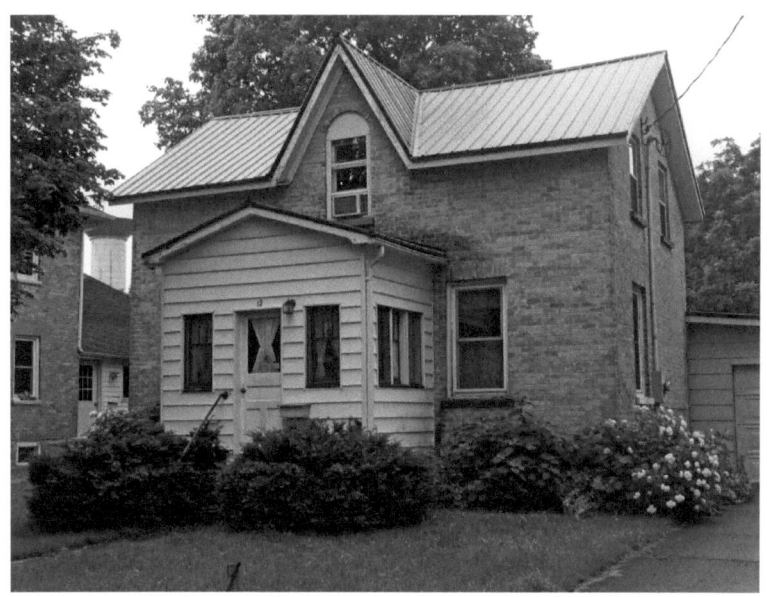

#12 - Gothic Revival – yellow brick

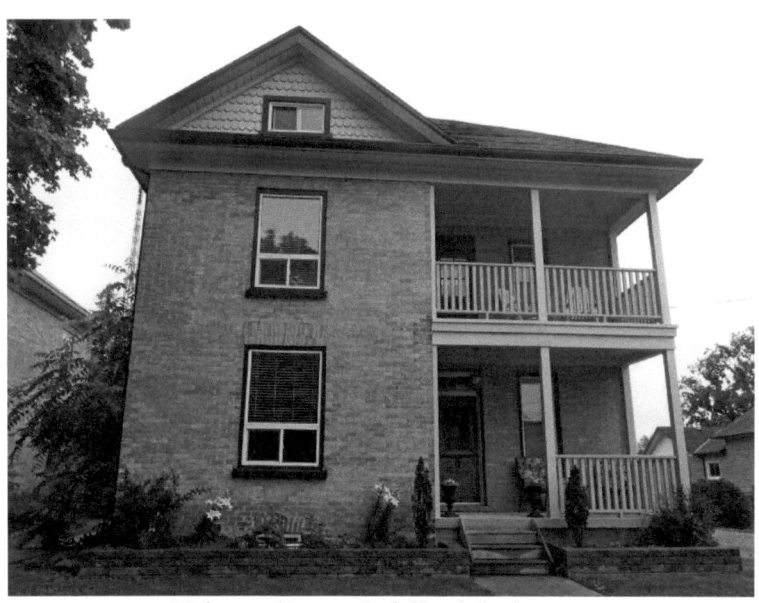

Edwardian – 2nd floor balcony

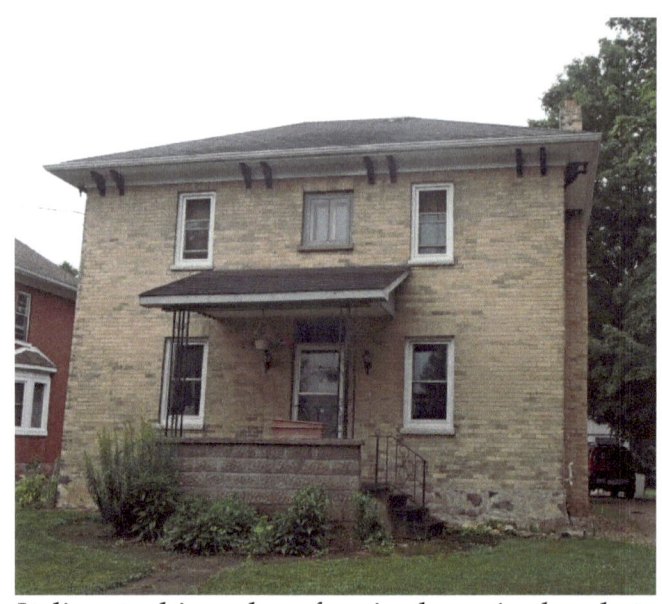

Italianate, hipped roof, paired cornice brackets

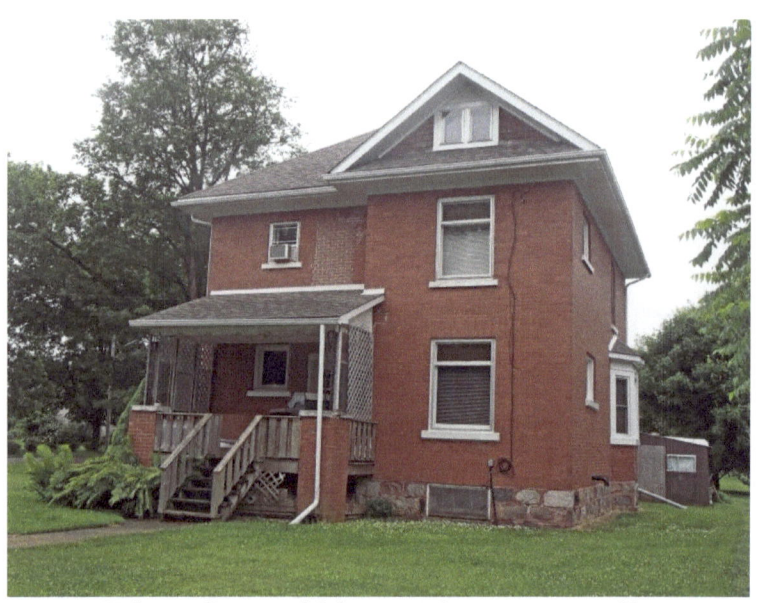

Edwardian, cobblestone basement walls

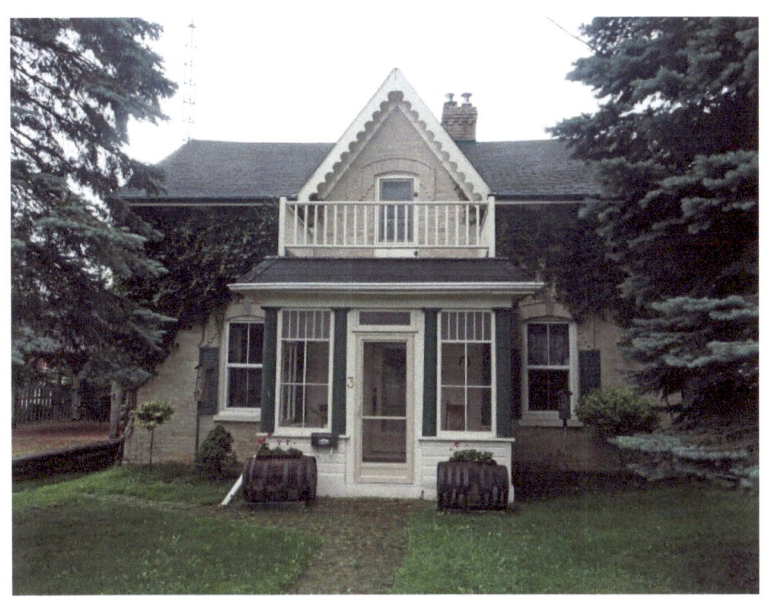

#3 – Gothic Revival – verge board trim on gable,
2nd floor balcony

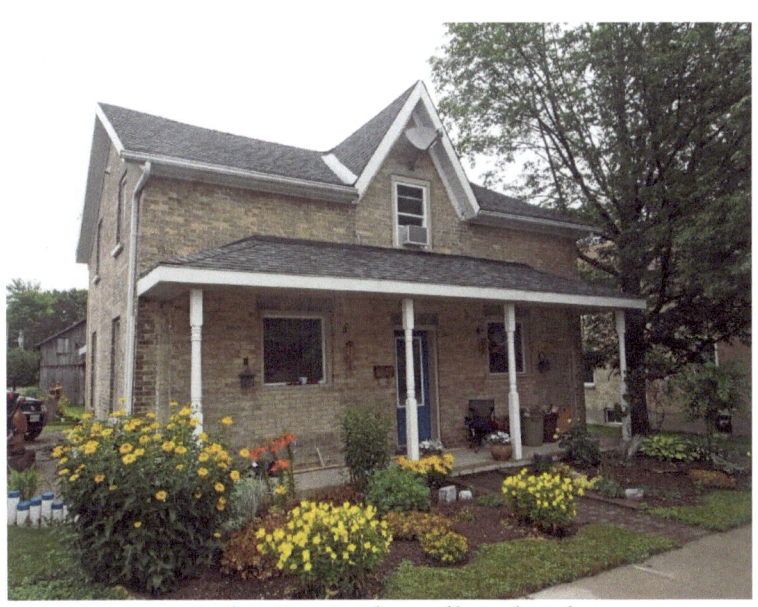

Gothic Revival – yellow brick

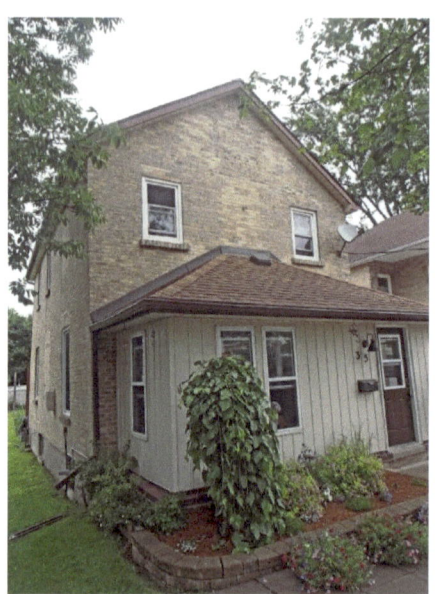

35 Elora Street – Gothic, yellow brick

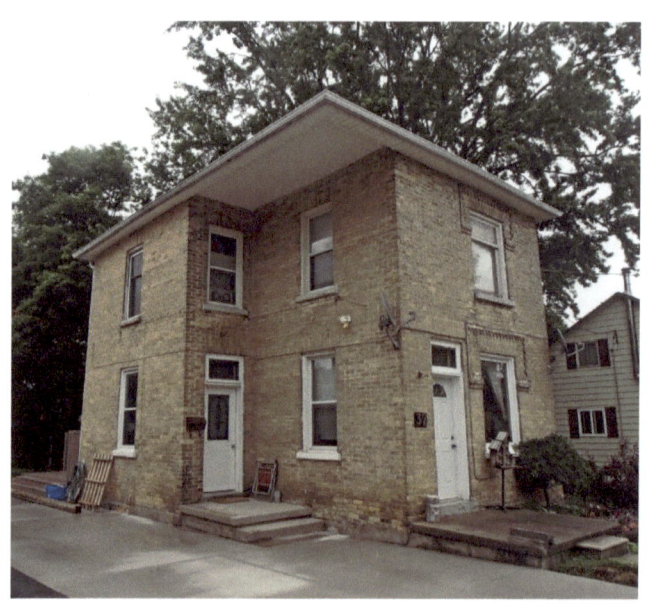

37 Elora Street – yellow brick

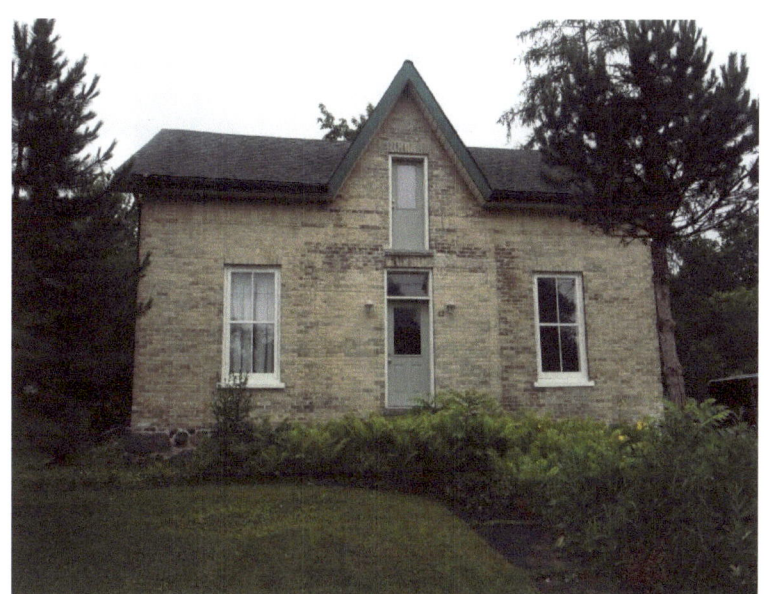

42 Elora Street - Gothic Revival – yellow brick

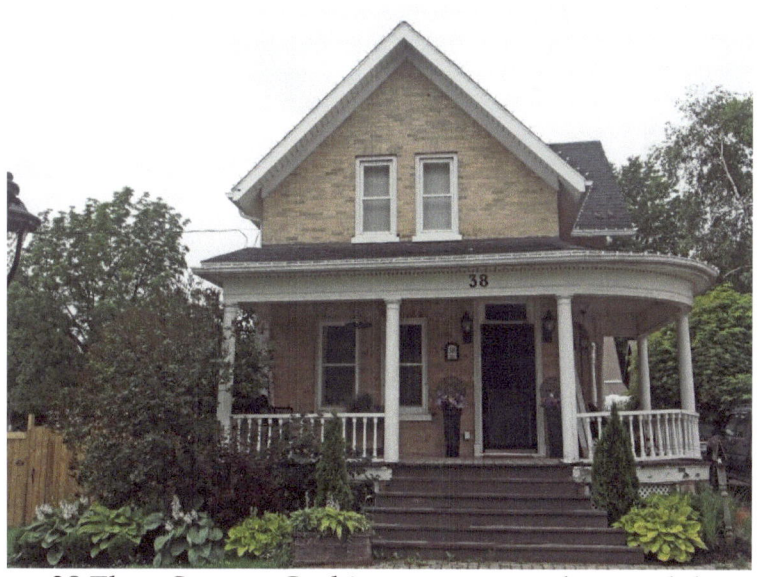

38 Elora Street – Gothic - wraparound verandah

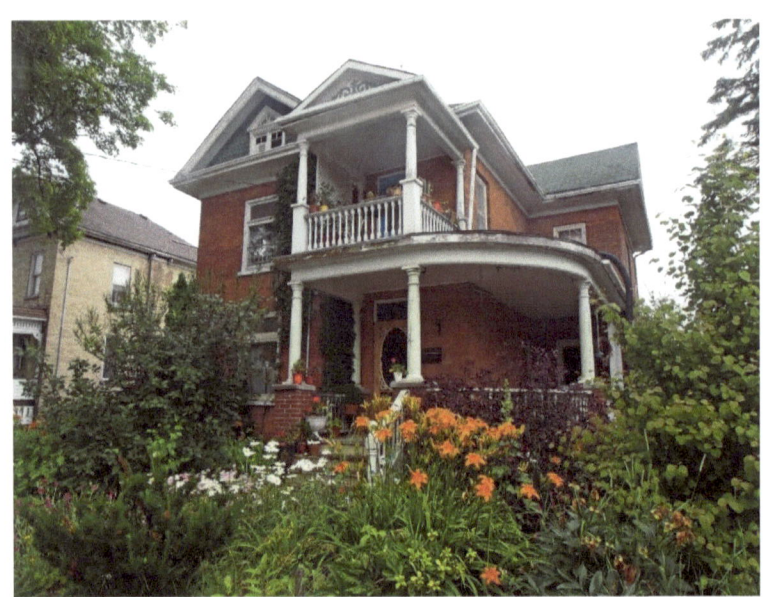

Edwardian – wraparound verandah, balcony on second floor, pediment

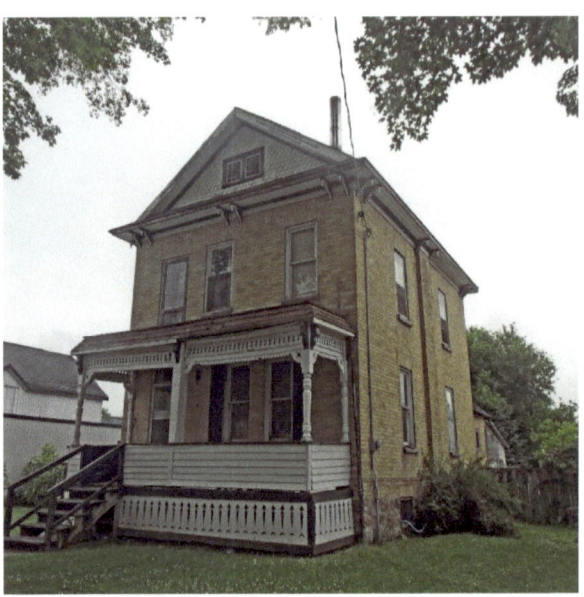

Gothic Revival - paired cornice brackets

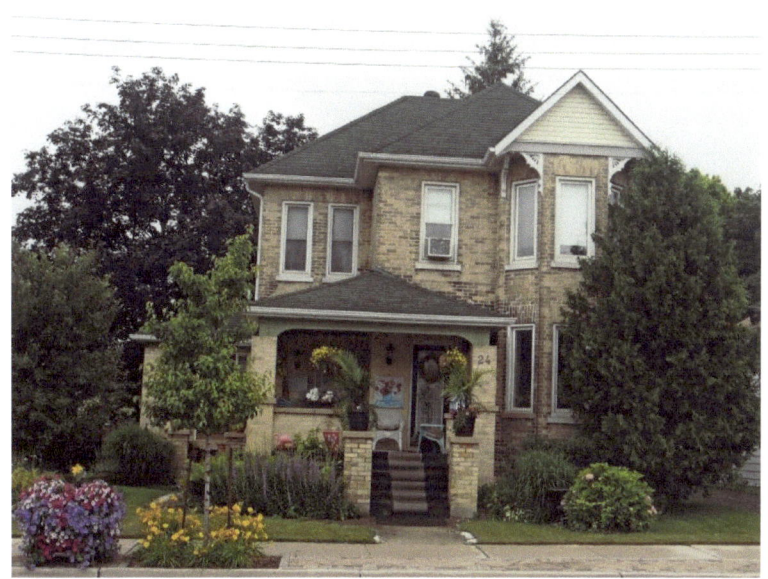

24 Elora Street – fretwork, two-storey bay window

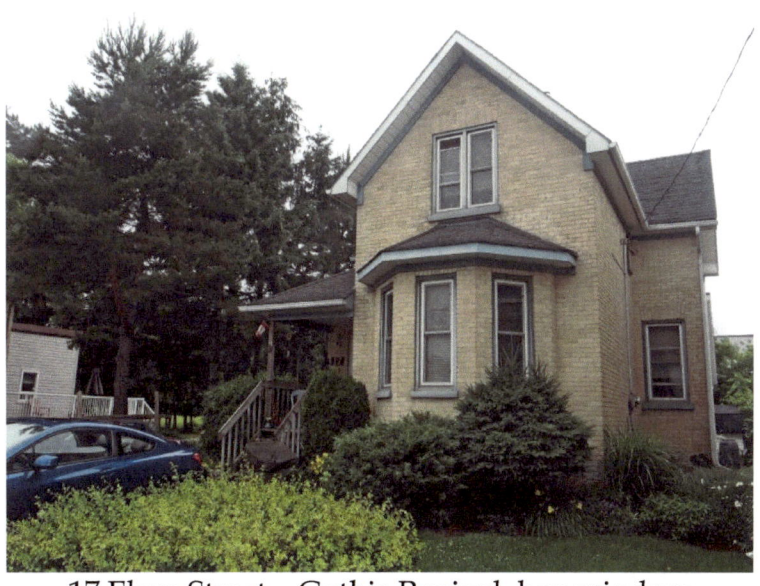

17 Elora Street – Gothic Revival, bay window

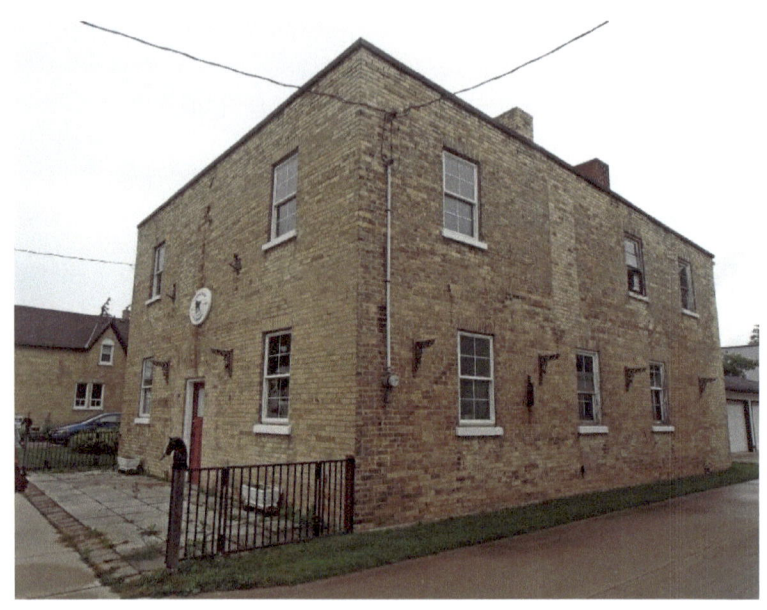

#19 - Original blacksmith shop c. 1904

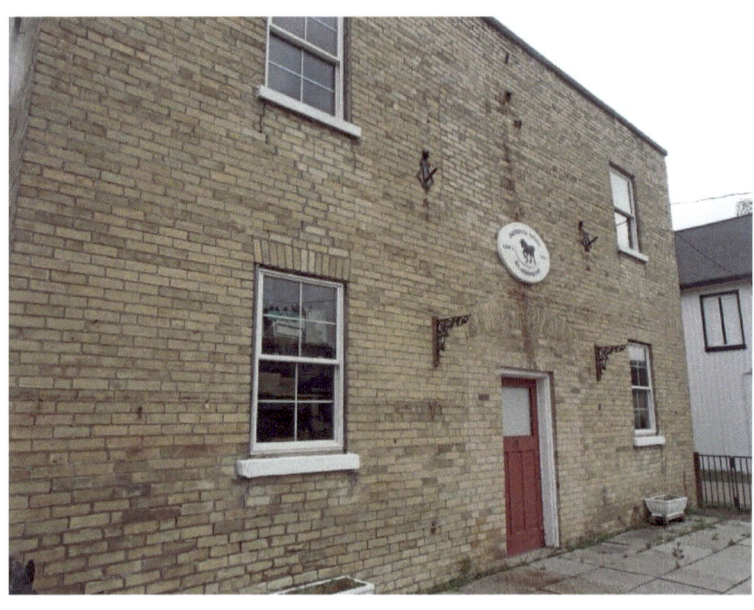

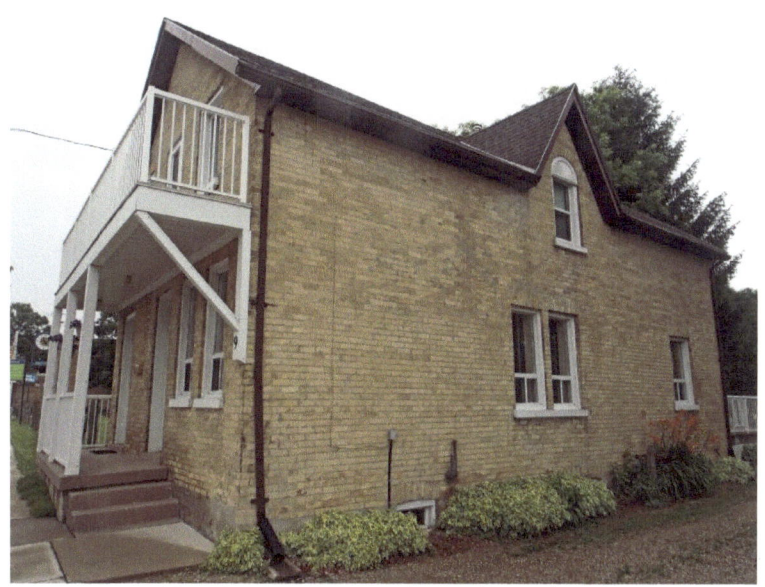

#9 - Gothic Revival – yellow brick

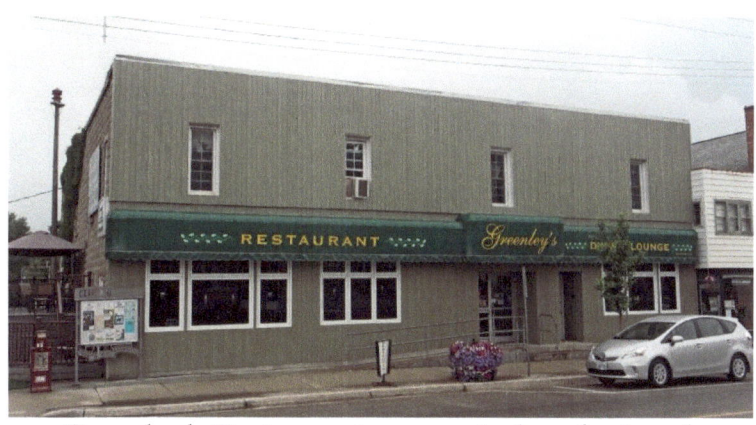

Greenley's Restaurant – a great place for lunch

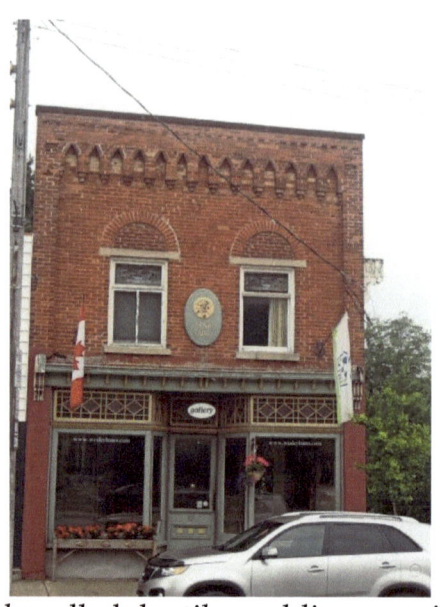

Red brick – bevelled dentil moulding, cornice brackets, window voussoirs

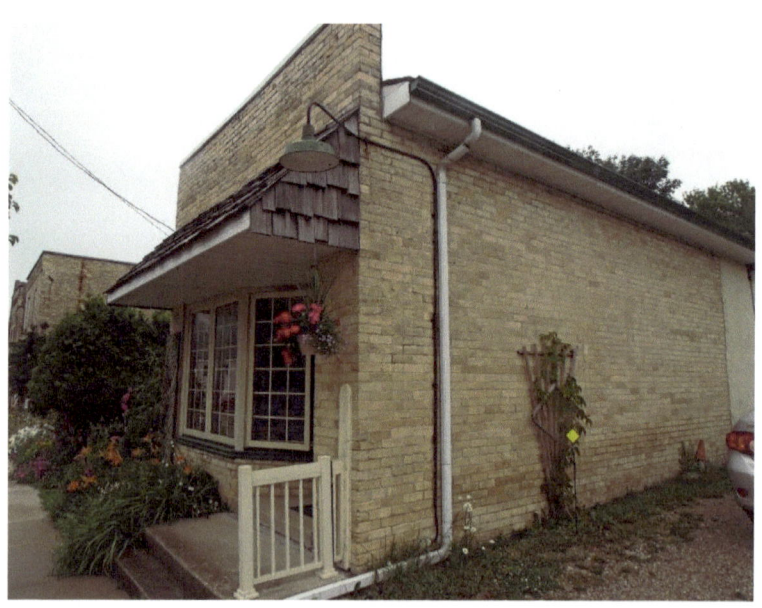

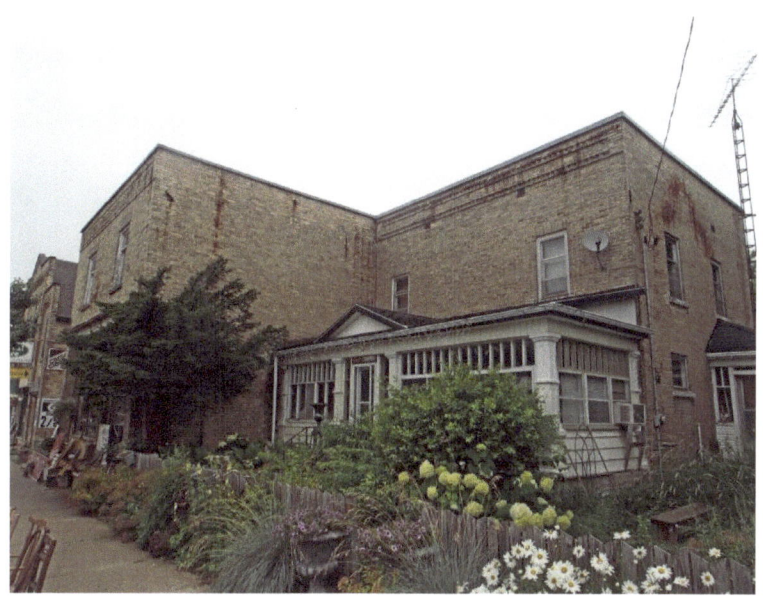

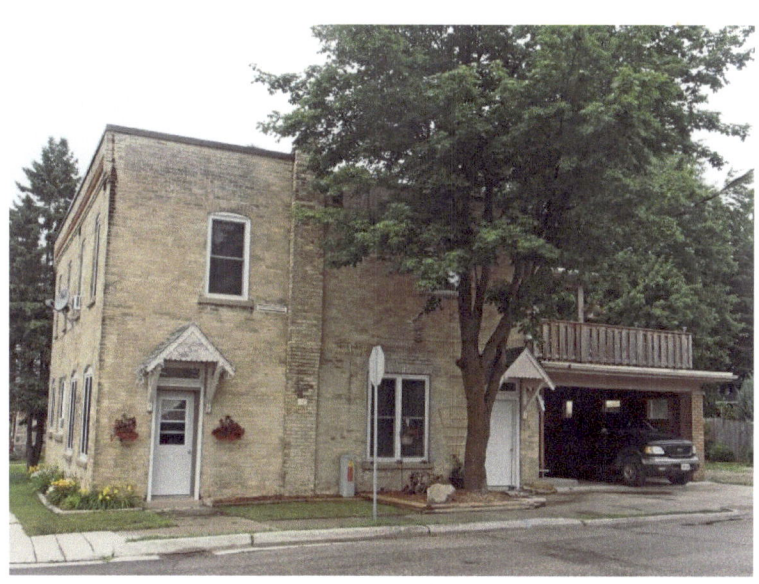

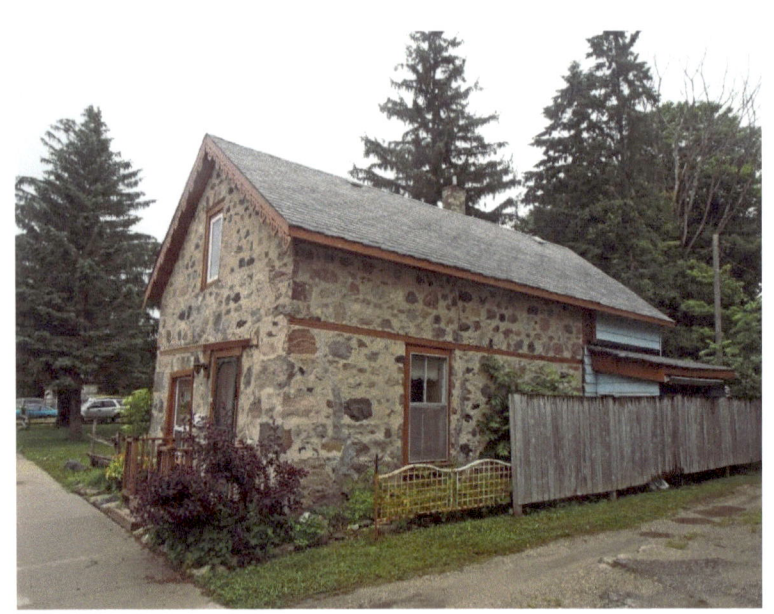

Cobblestone architecture

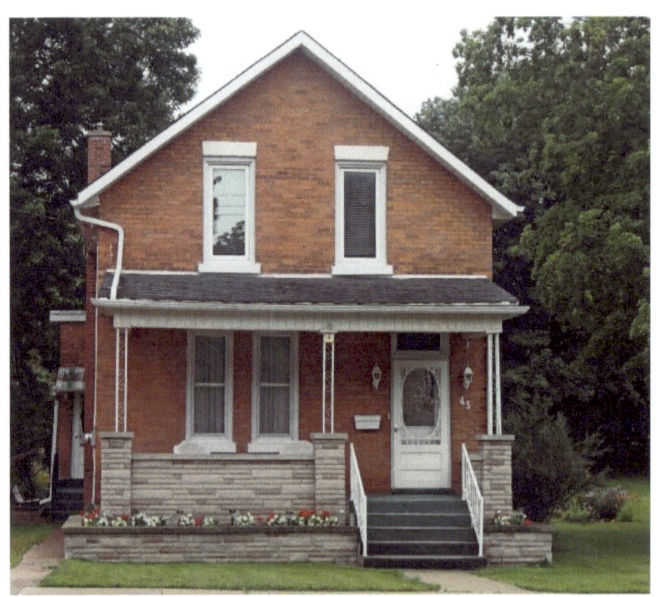

#45 – red brick, Gothic Revival

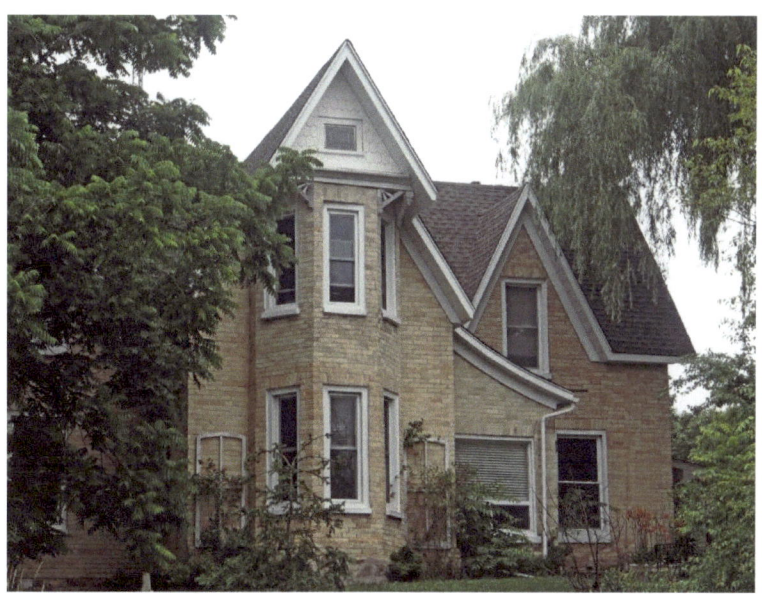

Gothic Revival – two-storey bay window

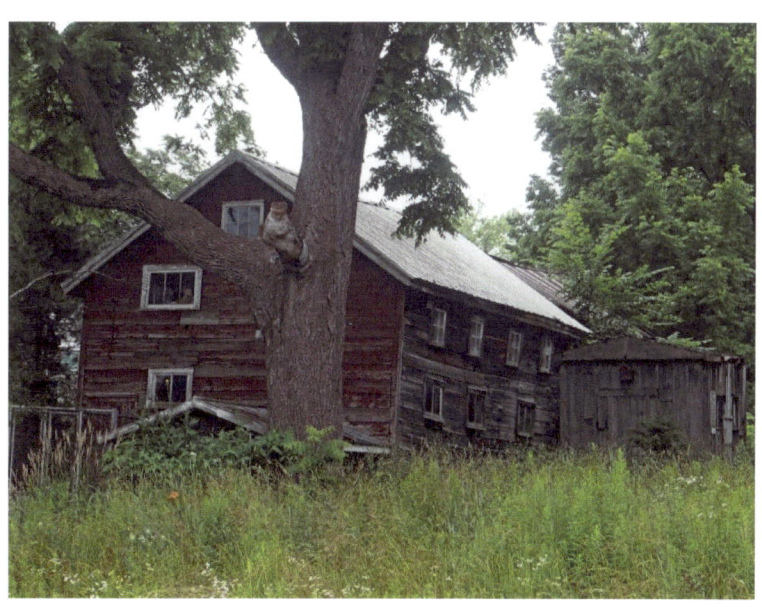

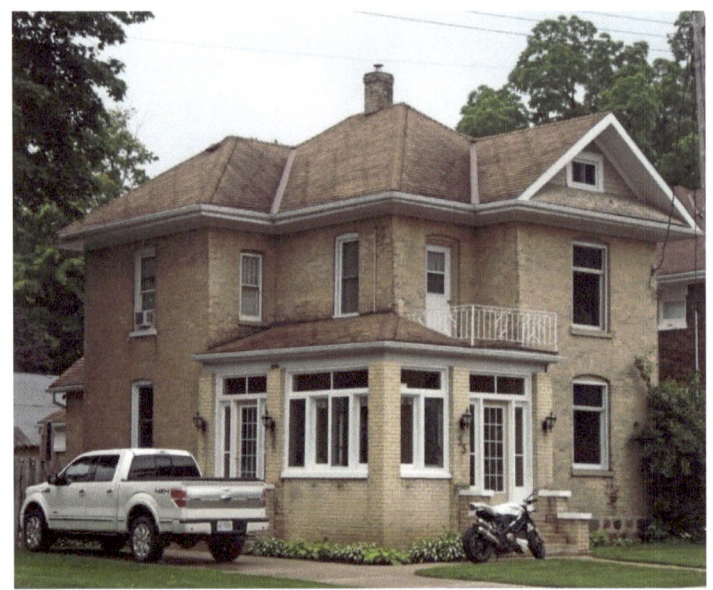

Edwardian style - second floor balcony

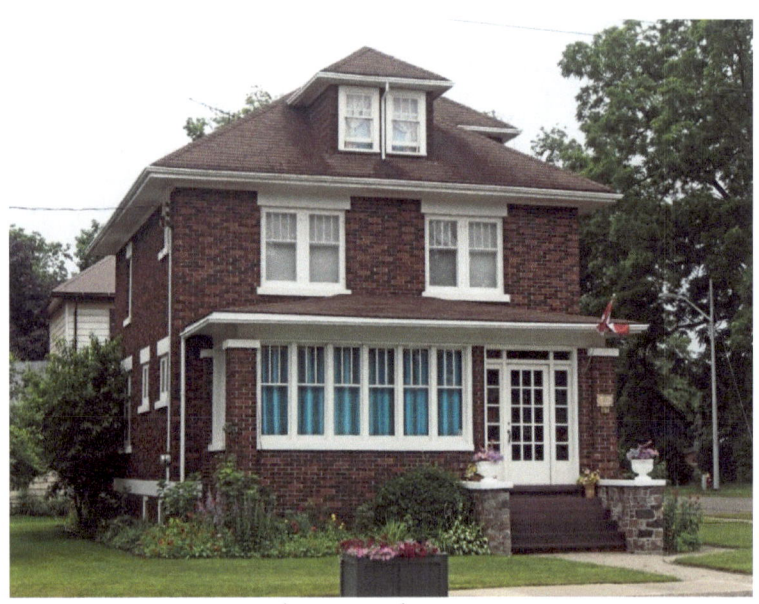

#57 - Italianate, dormer in attic

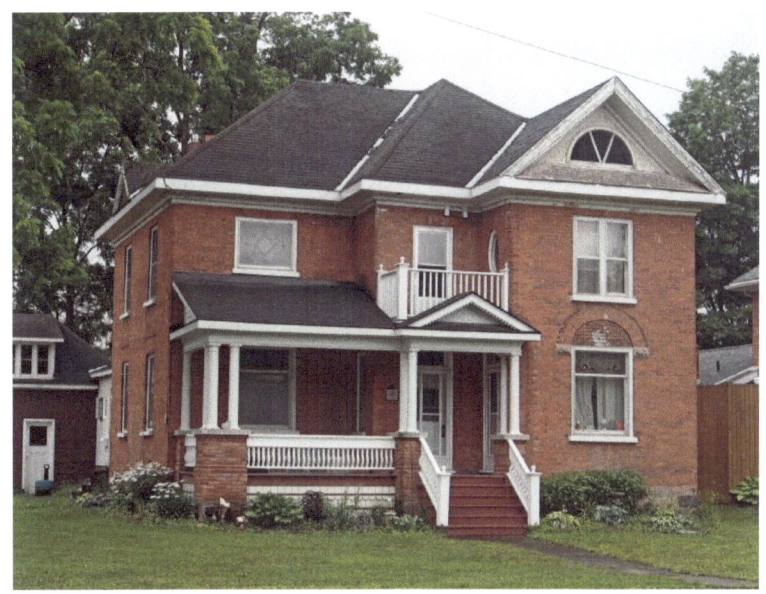

1867 – Clifford Heritage Building, pediment, 2nd floor balcony

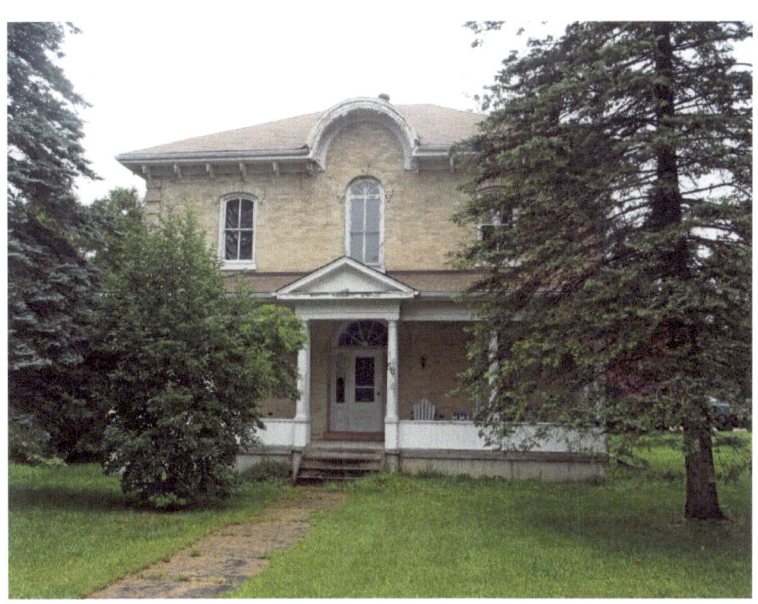

#58 - Italianate, pediment

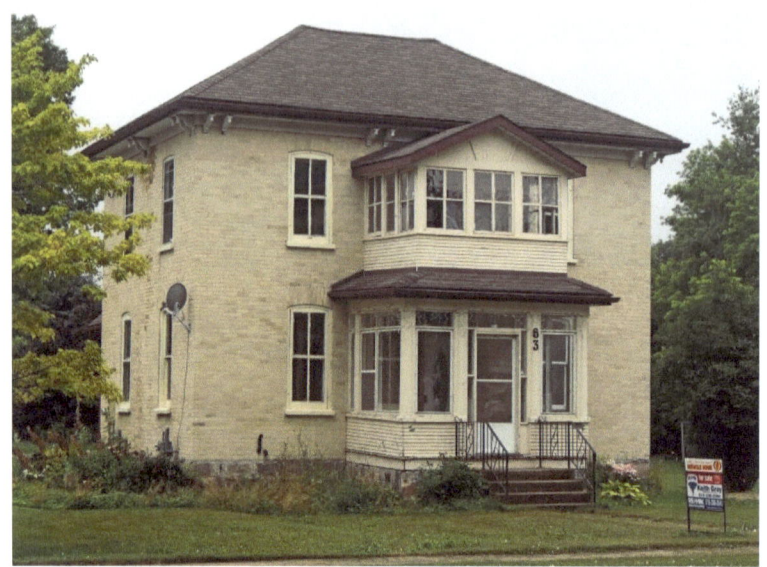

#63 – Italianate – hipped roof

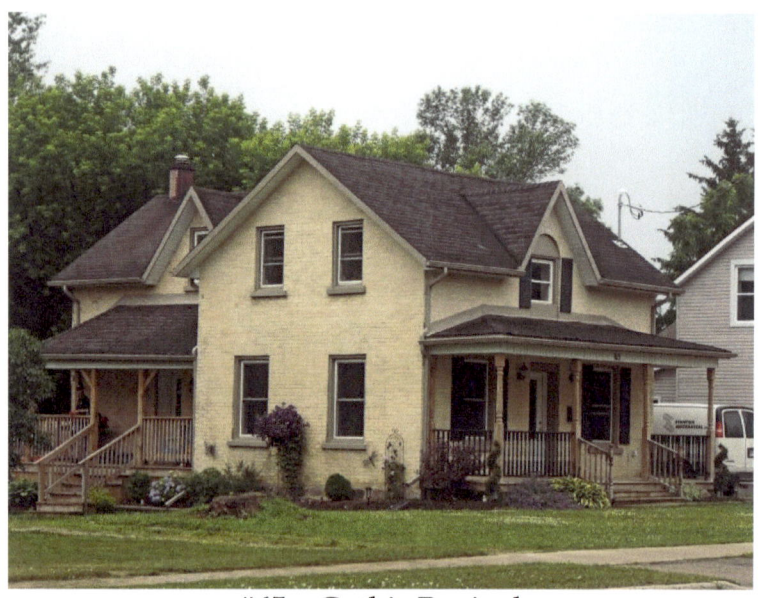

#65 – Gothic Revival

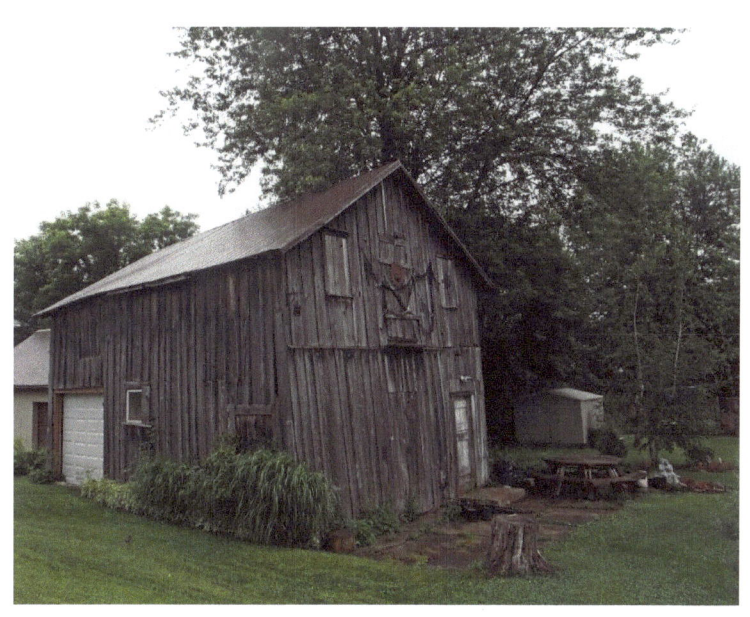

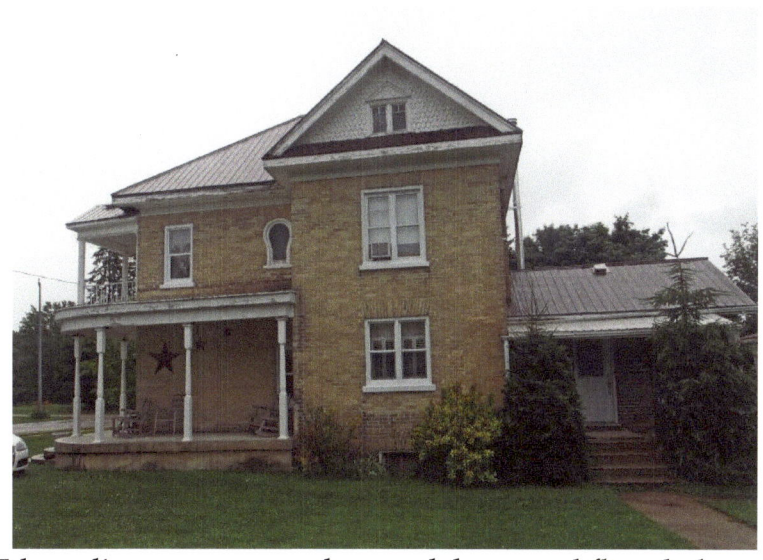

Edwardian, wraparound verandah, second floor balcony,
Keyhole window

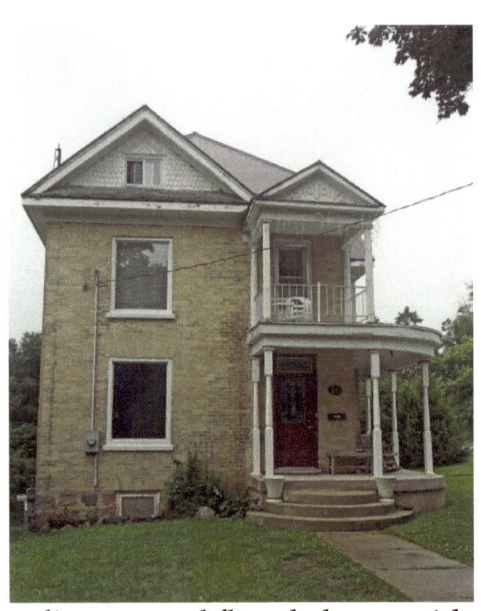

#16 - Edwardian, second floor balcony with pediment, wraparound verandah

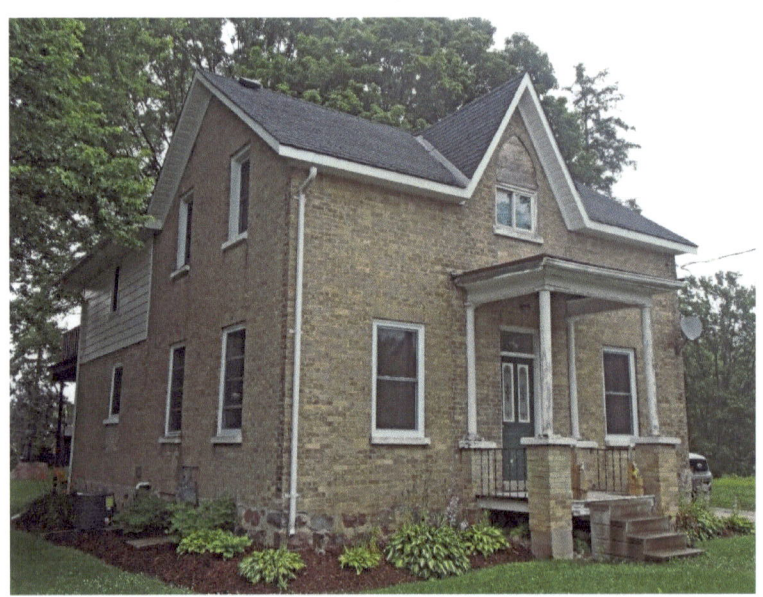

Gothic Revival

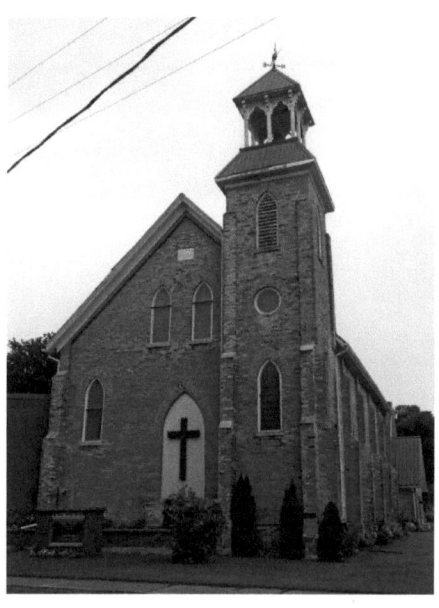

Knox United Church, corner of William Street

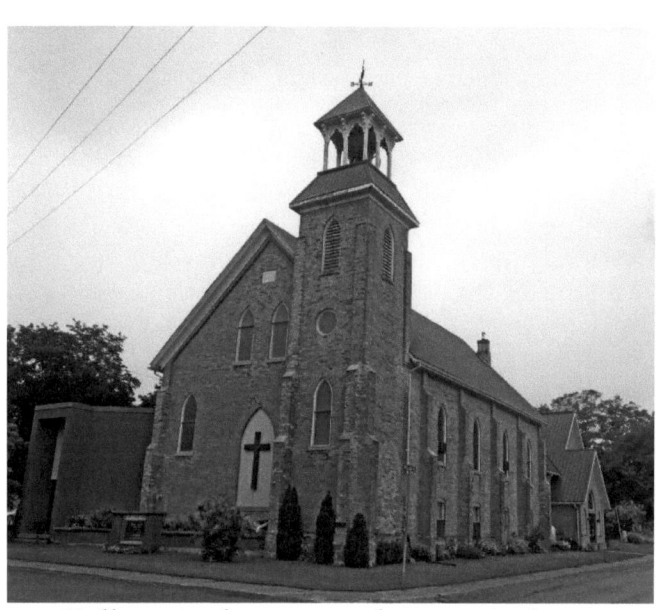

Bell tower, buttresses, lancet windows

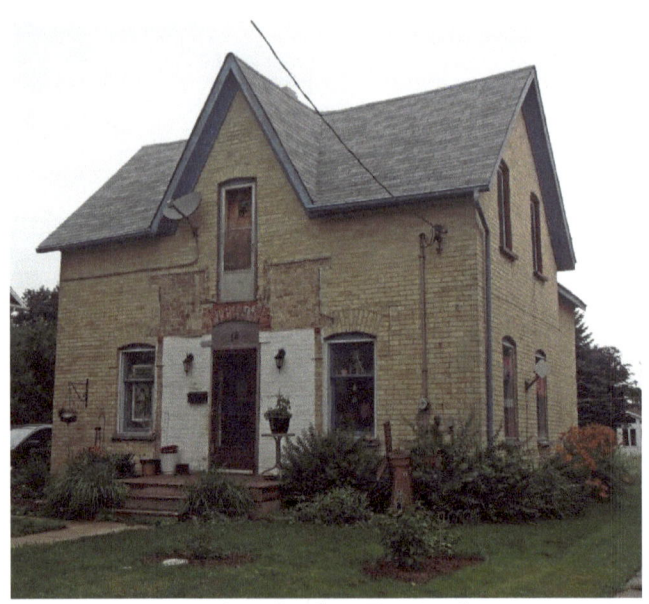

#18 – Gothic Revival

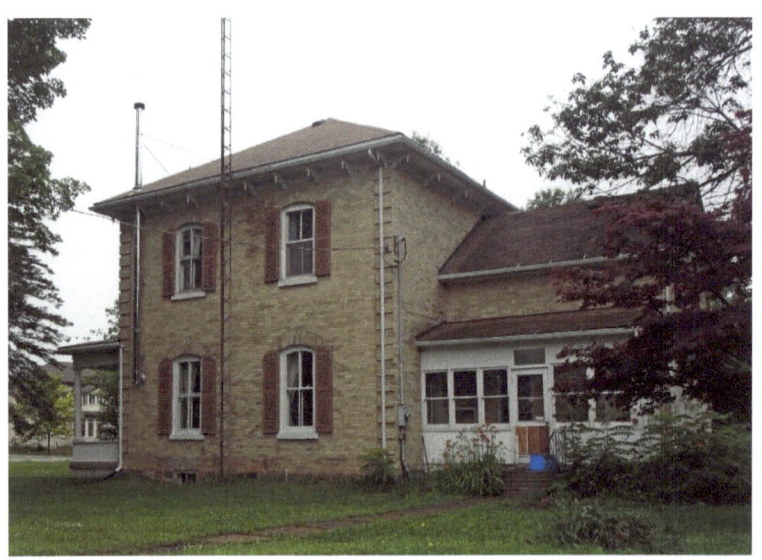

Italianate, cornice brackets, hipped roof

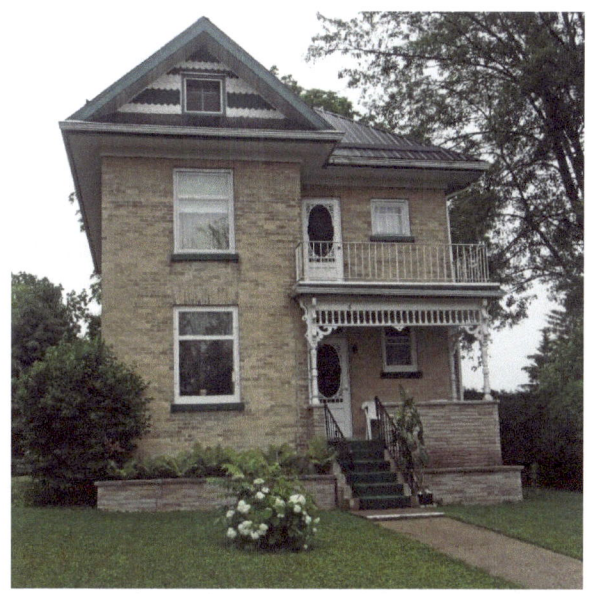

#6 – Edwardian, second floor balcony

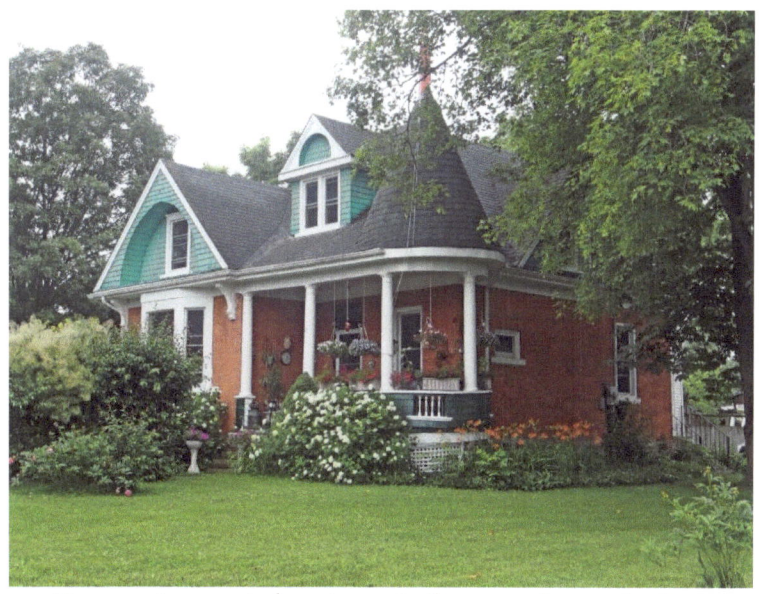

Queen Anne style – turret, dormer, bay window

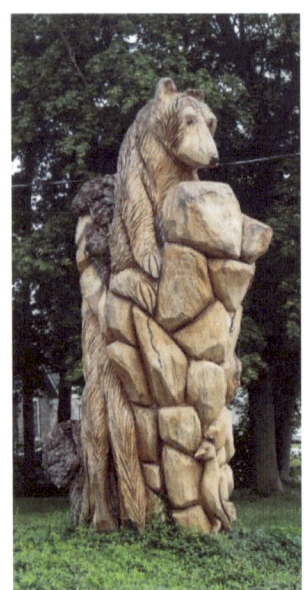
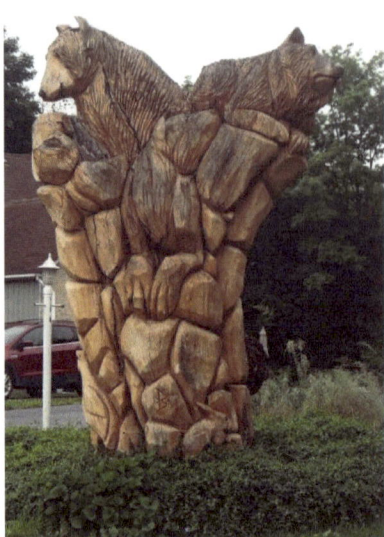

Bear carvings

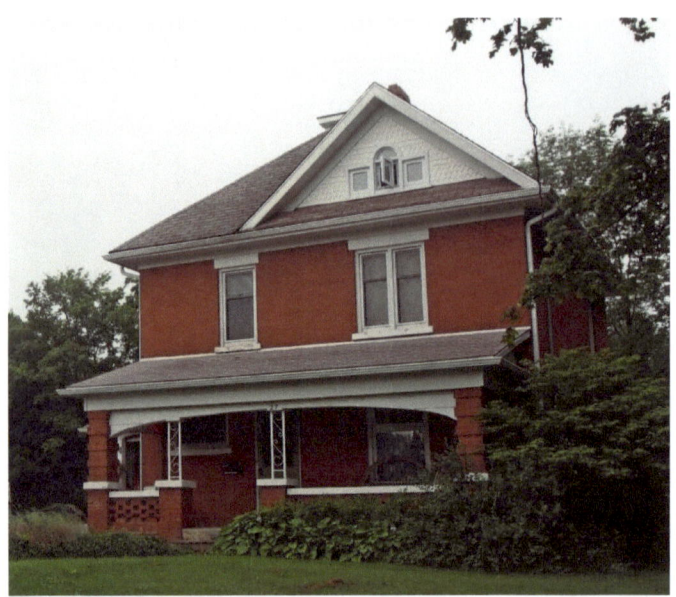

#27 - Edwardian – Palladian window

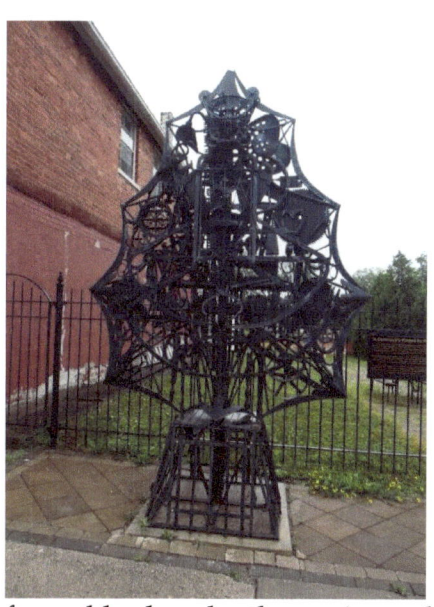

A community forged by hand – the various elements in this sculpture are the common artifacts of daily life representing ancestors and their work as individuals which in turn created the community.

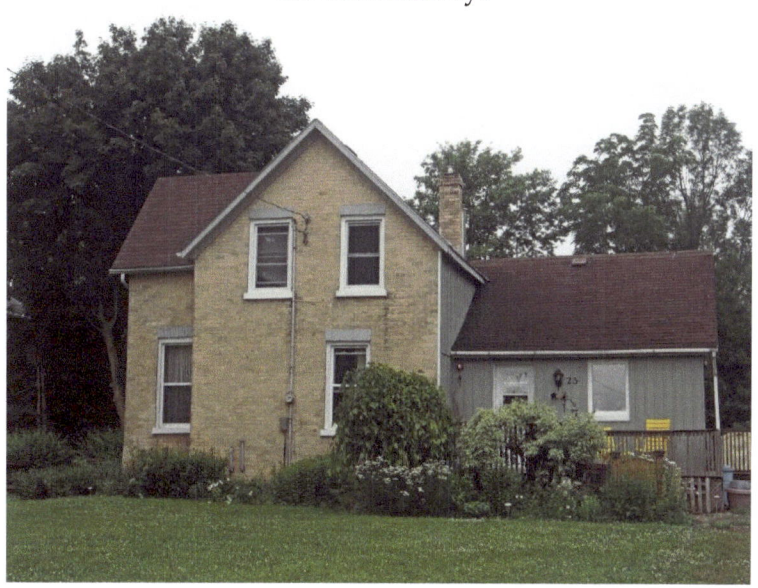

#25 – Gothic Revival

Bay Window: A window that projects out from a wall, in a semicircular, rectangular, or polygonal design. Used frequently in Gothic and Victorian designs. Example: Clifford – see Page 37	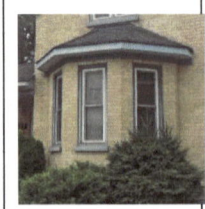
Brackets: a decorative or weight-bearing structural element which forms a right angle with one side against a wall and the other under a projecting surface such as an eave or roof. Example: Clifford – see Page 40	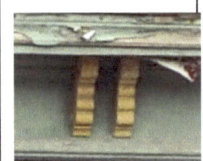
Buttress: a masonry structure built against or projecting from a wall which serves to support or reinforce the wall. In Canadian architecture, they are sometimes used for decoration. Example: Knox Presbyterian Church – see Page 8	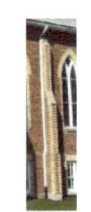
Cobblestone architecture: Refers to the use of cobblestones embedded in mortar as a method for erecting walls on houses and commercial buildings. Example: Clifford – see Page 25	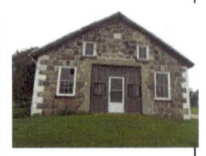
Cupola: A domed or curved roof rising from a building as a decorative element. Example: see Page 21	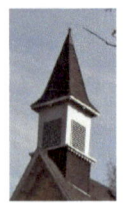

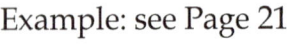

Dentil Moulding: an even series of rectangles used as ornamental decoration in cornices. Example: see Page 24	
Dichromatic brickwork: the use of two colours of brick, tile or slate to decorate a façade. Example: Clifford – see Page 27	
Dormer: (French for "sleep") a gable end window that pierces through the plane of a sloping roof surface to create usable space in the top floor or attic of a building by adding headroom. Example: Clifford – see Page 44	
Fretwork: interlaced decorative design resembling a bracket Example: see Page 8	
Gable: the triangular portion of a wall between the edges of a sloping roof. Example: Clifford – see Page 33	
Hipped Roof: a roof where all sides slope downwards to the walls with no gables. Example: Harrison – see Page 16	
Lancet Window: a tall, narrow window with a pointed arch at its top. Example: see Page 27	

Palladian Window: a large window that is divided into three sections with the centre section larger than the two side sections and usually arched. Example: Clifford – see Page 30	
Pediment: a triangular section above the horizontal structure (entablature), typically supported by columns. The inside of the triangle is called the tympanum. Example: Harrison – see Page 9	
Quoin: masonry blocks at the corner of a wall, often a decorative feature, usually larger or of a different colour than the rest of the wall. Example: see Page 10	
Turret: a small tower that projects from the wall of a building. Example: see Page 51	
Vergeboard and Finial: also called bargeboards – hang from the projecting end of a roof and are often elaborately carved and ornamented. **Finial:** ornament added to the top of a gable, pinnacle, canopy or spire – a Gothic element. Example: See Page 14	
Voussoirs: is a wedge-shaped element used in building an arch. A keystone is the central stone that locks all the stones into position, allowing the arch to bear weight. Example: see Page 40	

Building Styles

Edwardian, 1900-1930 – This style bridges the ornate and elaborate styles of the Victorian era and the simplified styles of the 20th century. Balanced facades, simple roof lines, dormer windows, large front porches, and smooth brick surfaces are its characteristics. Example: Harrison – see Page 9	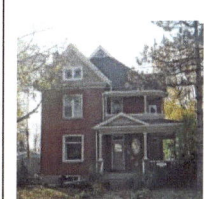
Gothic Revival, 1830-1890 – These decorative buildings have sharply-pitched gables with highly detailed verge boards, pointed-arch window openings, and dichromatic brickwork. It is a common style in Ontario. Example: Harrison – see Page 23	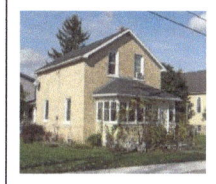
Italianate, 1850-1900 – It has wide-bracketed eaves, belvederes, wrap-around verandahs. Example: Clifford – see Page 30	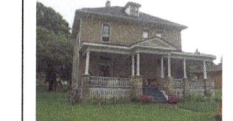
Queen Anne, 1885-1900 – This style is distinguished by an irregular outline featuring a combination of an offset tower, broad gables, projecting two-storey bays, verandahs, multi-sloped roofs, and tall, decorative chimneys. A mixture of brick and wood is common. Windows often have one large single-paned bottom sash and small panes in the upper sash. Example: Clifford – see Page 51	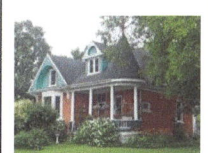

www.ingramcontent.com/pod-product-compliance
Lightning Source LLC
Chambersburg PA
CBHW040855180526
45159CB00001B/431